A Spiritual
Warfare
Discussion
M...

THE
GREAT
WAR

God, Satan and You

by Dawson McAllister
and Rich Miller

Printed in the United States of America   ISBN 0-923417-21-4

Research and Author Assistant: **Tim Altman**
Editor and Publication Director: **Wayne Peterson**
Illustrator: **Kim Trammell/LOC Graphics**

SHEPHERD MINISTRIES
2845 W. Airport Freeway, Suite 137
Irving, Texas 75062
(214) 570-7599

Dawson McAllister

Dawson McAllister is one of America's outstanding youth communicators. He has been a youth pastor, coffee house counselor, author, TV and radio host and friend to thousands of teenagers.

After academic study at Bethel College in Minnesota and Talbot Theological Seminary in California, Dawson became involved in a program for runaways and desperate teenagers that has developed into a nation-wide ministry. His practical experience and spiritual insight make him much in demand as a speaker at assemblies, weekend seminars, conferences and camps.

A series of prime time TV specials entitled "Kids in Crisis" has enabled him to provide spiritual counsel to teenage youth throughout the nation. And now, an ongoing tool to reach the American teenager is live call-in radio entitled, "Dawson McAllister Live." This one-hour weekly satellite program brings troubled, confused teenagers into contact with straight talk and clear Biblical guidance.

Fifteen popular discussion manuals, thirteen video programs and a film series have multiplied his ministry to individuals and small groups.

Dawson lives with his wife and two sons on an historic farm outside of Nashville, Tennessee, where he enjoys breaking and training horses in his spare time.

Rich Miller

Rich Miller is a vibrant, athletic youth leader who has been associated with Campus Crusade for sixteen years working with high school students. He originally planned to be a weather forecaster and took his BS degree from Penn State in meteorology.

One outstanding experience in Rich's career was the year he spent traveling with Josh McDowell. In 1980 he went to California and earned a master's degree in Christian apologetics at the Simon Greenleaf School of Law in Anaheim. He also has written for Campus Life magazine.

Rich Miller lives in Warminster, outside of Philadelphia, and enjoys an active life of sports—racquetball, tennis, golf, swimming and running. But his real vocation is working with high school students, telling them about Jesus Christ and the satisfying life which He offers.

Rich and his wife Shirley are presently ministering with Campus Crusade in Manila, Philippines, where he is heading up a special evangelism project.

God...

Satan...

and You

The Great War

Contents

Use Of This Manual

THE GREAT WAR is a study and discussion tool for individuals, one-on-one counseling, youth groups, weekend conferences, seminars and week-long camps.

THE GREAT WAR is a teaching manual to challenge the thinking student who is looking for answers. It is an excellent resource for the youth leader who is seeking to develop the faith and commitment of students.

Scripture passages in this manual are highlighted to call attention to their importance and to make them stand out from the context. The Bible is our ultimate resource in life and is the heart of this study. Various versions are used to bring out the vital teaching of each passage and to communicate clearly what God says!

The questions are designed to motivate thoughtful discussion, make significant points clearly understandable and to apply Scripture to the individual in current experience.

The planned progression of this study makes it important for the youth leader and the student to follow the chapter topics in succession, at least for the first time.

Introduction

The day we accepted Christ, many amazing things happened to us. For example:

—Jesus came into our lives and gave us eternal life.
—We were forgiven of all our sins.
—We were empowered to live a whole new kind of life.
—We began to love and care for other Christians.

However, we soon realized that something else was happening to us. We really began to struggle with what we knew God expected of us. Perhaps some of the evidences of this struggle were these:

—Reading our Bible and praying gradually became harder to do.
—We often seemed too tired, too busy or too distracted to spend quality
    time with God.
—The idea of sharing our faith made us uneasy and maybe a little
    resentful.
—We've made commitments to do better in our Christian lives, but
    somehow keep coming up short.

Why do we have these struggles? Why do our lives often seem like a war zone? Why does each day tend to feel like the start of a new battle?

The painful truth is that we are in the middle of a great spiritual war between God's Kingdom and Satan's Kingdom. And though there are no guns or bullets, it is still a violent life and death struggle that affects all of us—Christians and non-Christians alike.

Though we may find it hard to believe, this spiritual war rages around us each day and can cause horrible destruction in our lives. However, we don't need to be afraid. God loves us. Therefore, He wants to protect us and equip us so that we can personally experience the great victory which He has already won for us through Christ.

IN THIS BOOK, WE WILL LEARN ABOUT THE REAL SPIRITUAL WAR BEING FOUGHT BETWEEN THE KINGDOM OF GOD AND THE KINGDOM OF SATAN. WE WILL LEARN HOW THE WAR BEGAN, HOW CHRIST DEFEATED SATAN, AND WHY SATAN IS STILL A DANGEROUS ENEMY WHO WE MUST DEFEND AGAINST EACH DAY!

---

1 | Who Is Satan?

1 Who Is Satan?

The Bible teaches that we are involved in a major spiritual war. That war is between the Kingdom of God and the Kingdom of Satan. However, in order for us to understand this war we must first understand more about this mysterious creature called Satan. Where did he come from? Why is he so powerful? What led him to start a war with God?

IN THIS CHAPTER, WE WILL DISCUSS
WHAT SATAN WAS LIKE, WHY HE
REBELLED AGAINST GOD, AND WHAT
GOD DID ABOUT HIS REBELLION.

1 | Who Is Satan?

I. WHAT WAS SATAN LIKE?

The Bible has much to say about Satan as we can see from Ezekiel 28.

Ezekiel 28:12-17 (NIV)

12) "Son of man, take up a lament concerning the king of Tyre and say to him: 'This is what the Sovereign Lord says: "'You were the model of perfection, full of wisdom and perfect in beauty.

13) You were in Eden, the garden of God; every precious stone adorned you: ruby, topaz and emerald, chrysolite, onyx and jasper, sapphire, turquoise and beryl. Your settings and mountings were made of gold; on the day you were created they were prepared.

14) You were anointed as a guardian cherub, for so I ordained you. You were on the holy mount of God; you walked among the fiery stones.

15) You were blameless in your ways from the day you were created till wickedness was found in you.

16) Through your widespread trade you were filled with violence, and you sinned. So I drove you in disgrace from the mount of God, and I expelled you, O guardian cherub, from among the fiery stones.

17) Your heart became proud on account of your beauty, and you corrupted your wisdom because of your splendor. So I threw you to the earth; I made a spectacle of you before kings.

Who Is Satan? | *1*

In Ezekiel 28:1-11, God is giving a message to the prophet about a godless king who lived in Old Testament times. He refers to this king as the prince of Tyre. However, in verse twelve, God directs His message to another person, whom He calls the King of Tyre. This king is actually an evil spiritual power who controls the human prince of Tyre. This evil king is none other than Satan, himself. God begins His message to Satan by speaking through the prophet Ezekiel. He says, *"Son of man, take up a lament concerning the King of Tyre."* The word *"lament"* is a very powerful word. It means "a funeral song", "a heart-rending song of sadness." It has the idea of crying and sobbing in grief because of a broken heart. It is obvious from verse 12 that Satan has broken God's heart. How did this happen? To learn the truth, we must go back to the very beginning of Satan's life.

A. THE QUALITIES OF SATAN

Most people think of Satan as a dark, ugly and evil creature. While this is true in part, Satan did not start out that way. He was an awesome example of God's creativity. Ezekiel 28:12-13 gives us a picture of the incredible qualities God created in Satan.

> Ezekiel 28:12-13 (NIV)
> *12) "Son of man, take up a lament concerning the king of Tyre and say to him: 'This is what the Sovereign Lord says: "'You were the model of perfection, full of wisdom and perfect in beauty.*
> *13) You were in Eden, the garden of God; every precious stone adorned you: ruby, topaz and emerald, chrysolite, onyx and jasper, sapphire, turquoise and beryl. Your settings and mountings were made of gold; on the day you were created they were prepared.*

1 | Who Is Satan?

SATAN WAS A MODEL OF PERFECTION

Ezekiel 28:12 lets us know that Satan was a *"model of perfection."* What do you think this means?

_____

_____

_____

When verse 12 calls Satan a model of perfection, it means that he could not be improved upon. He was so perfect that all other angels could be modeled after him. When car companies decide to build a new kind of car they make many trial models. These trial models are called prototypes. Eventually, they build the perfect prototype, which they use as a model for mass-producing many more just like it. In a somewhat similar way, Satan was a perfect prototype Angel, the Ultimate of God's creation. There was none greater, except God, Himself.

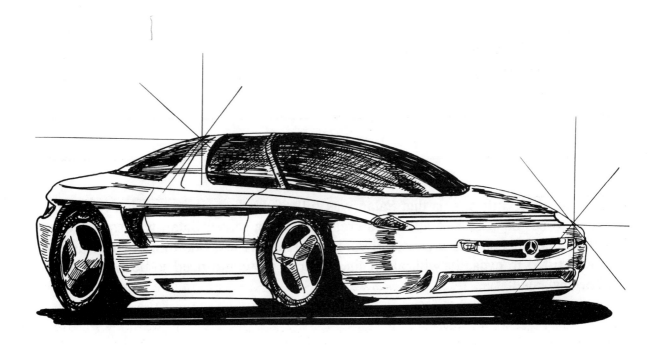

Who Is Satan?

SATAN WAS FULL OF WISDOM

Verse 12 also says that Satan was *"full of wisdom."* What do you think this means?

_____

_____

_____

When the Bible informs us that Satan was full of wisdom, it means that he was created to be the wisest of all God's creations. In a sense, Satan was so full of wisdom that he was like a cup that would overflow if just one more drop was added. He was filled to capacity with all of the wisdom he would need to be God's most important angel.

Who Is Satan?

SATAN WAS PERFECT IN BEAUTY

The Bible says Satan was *"perfect in beauty."* What do you think this means?

_____

_____

_____

Verse 12 concludes by stating that Satan was perfect in beauty. This means that Satan was clearly the most beautiful of God's creations. It was a fact that was beyond debate. Except for God, there has never been anyone more beautiful than Satan. Verse 13 gives us even more insight into his beauty by describing him as being covered with every kind of precious jewel.

> Ezekiel 28:13 (NIV)
> *13) You were in Eden, the garden of God; every precious stone adorned you: ruby, topaz and emerald, chrysolite, onyx and jasper, sapphire, turquoise and beryl. Your settings and mountings were made of gold; on the day you were created they were prepared.*

Satan sparkled with incredible brilliance. In fact, his original name, Lucifer, means "light from heaven" or "shining one." Using your imagination, look again at verse 13 and try to describe what you think Satan must have looked like.

SATAN WAS LIKE A BEAUTIFUL MUSICAL INSTRUMENT

We learn from verse 13 that, *"Your settings and mountings were made of gold,"* but the words, *"settings and mountings"*, can also be translated *"tambourines and flutes"*.... The Bible is drawing us a word picture that describes Satan as a sparkling and beautiful musical instrument that probably played praises to God. Satan's every word and action was to be like a beautiful song that spoke of and praised God's greatness.

In summary, Satan was the most wise and beautiful being ever created. His appearance was dazzling and magnificent. He was a walking advertisement for the awesomeness of God. Nothing else in all creation could compare to him. He was so perfect in every way that simply being in his presence would likely cause a celebration of God's incredible creativity.

B. THE AUTHORITY OF SATAN

God not only created Satan to be awesome in appearance, but He created him also to have great authority. It may be that God gave him more power and more privileges than any other created being. Ezekiel 28:14 tells us about his incredible authority.

Ezekiel 28:14 (NIV)
14) You were anointed as a guardian cherub, for so I ordained you. You were on the holy mount of God; you walked among the fiery stones.

Who Is Satan? | 1

SATAN WAS APPOINTED TO BE A HIGH-RANKING ANGEL

God created Satan as a *"guardian cherub."* The job of cherub was probably the highest ranking position which God could offer. Throughout the Bible cherubs seem to have the special task of protecting or ruling over part of God's creation. Genesis 3:24 demonstrates that cherubs guarded or ruled over the garden of Eden to keep sin out and protect God's holiness. Ezekiel 28:14 makes it clear that God created Satan to be a guardian cherub. He was an incredibly powerful angel who was given the authority to rule over and protect whatever God put into his care.

SATAN HAD FACE-TO-FACE ACCESS TO GOD

Ezekiel 28:14 tells us that Satan was *"on the holy mount of God."* What do you think the *"mount of God"* is?

_____

_____

_____

Throughout the Bible, mountains are used to represent places where God exercised His great authority and power. In this verse the *"mount of God"* represents the ultimate place of power from which God rules. It is a place of brilliant light (fiery stones). It is His royal court. For Satan to stand in this place means he was granted high honor and great authority. It is possible that Satan served as God's prime minister to all of creation. Any creature who viewed Satan in the presence of God would have clearly known that this mighty cherub had been given power and authority like no other in creation.

1 | Who Is Satan?

II. WHY DID SATAN REBEL AGAINST GOD?

As we have seen, Satan was indeed a magnificent creation. Yet, despite attaining the most privileged position of any created being, he made a horrible choice that not only broke God's heart, but plunged all of creation into a deadly spiritual war. He chose to rebel against the very God who had created him and given him all that he possessed.

A. SATAN'S REASON FOR REBELLING AGAINST GOD

The prophet Ezekiel tells us what it was that caused Satan to turn against God.

> Ezekiel 28:15 & 17 (NIV)
> *15) You were blameless in your ways from the day you were created till wickedness was found in you.*
> *17) Your heart became proud on account of your beauty, and you corrupted your wisdom because of your splendor. So I threw you to the earth; I made a spectacle of you before kings.*

According to verse 15, what did God find in Satan's heart?

_____

_____

_____

According to verse 17, what was the wickedness that came into Satan's heart?

_____

_____

_____

Satan, known as the father of lies, lied to himself. He actually thought that he himself was the source of his beauty, wisdom and authority. He refused to accept the fact that all of his greatness was from God. Therefore, he no longer wanted to submit to God's authority. In his pride he most likely reasoned, "One as wise as I ought to be God; one as beautiful as I ought to be worshipped and not to worship another."[1] Satan's incredible pride led to his rebellion and started a terrible war with God.

B. SATAN'S PLAN TO CARRY OUT HIS REBELLION AGAINST GOD

As we have seen, being filled with pride was Satan's main problem. As his pride grew, He determined to overthrow the government of heaven and seize control of all God's power. The prophet Isaiah helps us understand Satan's twisted plans as he attempted to complete his treacherous takeover of God's kingdom.

---

[1]J. Dwight Pentecost, <u>Your Adversary The Devil</u> (Grand Rapids: Zondervan Publishing House, 1969), p. 17.

1 | Who Is Satan?

> Isaiah 14:12-14 (NIV)
> *12) How you have fallen from heaven, O morning star, son of the dawn! You have been cast down to the earth, you who once laid low the nations!*
> *13) You said in your heart, "I will ascend to heaven; I will raise my throne above the stars of God; I will sit enthroned on the mount of assembly, on the utmost heights of the sacred mountain.*
> *14) I will ascend above the tops of the clouds; I will make myself like the Most High."*

How many times in verses 13 and 14 did Satan say "*I will*"?

_____

_____

_____

Five times Satan says, "*I will*" in these verses. What do you think is wrong with Satan's five "I wills"?

_____

_____

_____

From eternity past until the fall of Satan there was only one will--and that was the will of God. The entire creation was designed to work in perfect harmony as long as that creation submitted to the will of God. Satan, however, put another will into creation when he rebelled. He now chose to operate from his own will. Each of the "I wills" in Isaiah 14:13 and 14 is evidence of Satan's desire to have more and more power and to push God out of his life.

THE FIVE "I WILLS" OF SATAN

1. *I WILL ASCEND TO HEAVEN*

> Isaiah 14:13 (NIV)
> *13) You said in your heart,"I WILL ASCEND TO HEAVEN..."*

What do you think Satan meant when he said *"I will ascend to heaven"*?

Go to Gods office

As we have already seen, Satan was God's greatest created being. Because he was in such high command, he had access to the very presence of God. What a moving experience it must have been for Satan to enter into the grandeur of God's throne. And yet, he could only do so with God's permission. Because of Satan's pride, he no longer wanted to come to God's heaven by permission. He wanted to own it. He ..."wanted to move God off of His throne and occupy that throne as though it were rightfully his."[2] Satan wanted to storm heaven and take it as his own kingdom. That is what he meant when he said, *"I will ascend into heaven."*

---

[2]J. Dwight Pentecost, <u>Your Adversary The Devil</u> (Grand Rapids: Zondervan Publishing House, 1969), p. 22.

2. *I WILL RAISE MY THRONE ABOVE THE STARS OF GOD*

> Isaiah 14:13 (NIV)
> *13) You said in your heart, "I will ascend to heaven; I WILL RAISE MY THRONE ABOVE THE STARS OF GOD..."*

What do you think Satan meant when he said *"I will raise my throne above the stars of God"*?

_____

_____

_____

To understand Satan's second "I will," we must understand what Isaiah is referring to when he uses the phrase *"stars of God."* The stars of God here do not refer to the stars that hang in the sky, but rather to angelic beings. In Job 38:4-7, God tells us that these stars are actually angels. God had given Satan the job of overseeing all of the angels. This was a tremendous responsibility. It was a position of great power. Satan, however, did not create the angels, he merely ruled over them on God's behalf. The angels knew that Satan's orders to them were really God's orders. They clearly understood that God had the ultimate authority. Tragically, this was not enough for Satan. He wanted to replace God and rule the angels on his own. Satan wanted all of the angels to worship him and thereby join him in his rebellion against God.

3. *I WILL SIT ENTHRONED...*

> Isaiah 14:13 (NIV)
> *13) You said in your heart, "I will ascend to heaven, I will raise my throne above the stars of God; I WILL SIT ENTHRONED ON THE MOUNT OF ASSEMBLY, ON THE UTMOST HEIGHTS OF THE SACRED MOUNTAIN."*

What do you think Satan meant when he said, *"I will sit enthroned on the mount of assembly on the utmost heights of the sacred mountain"*?

_____

_____

_____

In order to understand Satan's third "I will" we must understand the meaning of several words and phrases. The word *"enthroned"* basically means "to sit as a ruler" or "one in authority." The phrase *"on the utmost height of the sacred mountain"* refers to the highest place of authority and rulership that exists (Isaiah 2:2, Psalm 48:1-2). Only God can rule from this place. The word *"assembly"* refers to all of creation (Psalm 89:5-7). While it is true that Satan was delegated tremendous authority to rule for God, and therefore had tremendous power, he wanted more. He wanted to sit on God's throne and rule over all of creation both in heaven and on earth.

4. *I WILL ASCEND ABOVE THE TOPS OF THE CLOUDS*

> Isaiah 14:13-14 (NIV)
> *13) You said in your heart, "I will ascend to heaven; I will raise my throne above the stars of God; I will sit enthroned on the mount of assembly on the utmost heights of the sacred mountain.*
> *14) I WILL ASCEND ABOVE THE TOPS OF THE CLOUDS..."*

What do you think Satan meant when he said, *"I will ascend above the tops of the clouds"*?

Look at the beauty

In Satan's fourth "I will," the phrase *"tops of the clouds"* has a very special meaning. Many times throughout the Bible God appeared to people in clouds. They were evidence of the beauty and the glory of God (Exodus 16:10, I Kings 8:10, Matthew 24:30). As we have already seen, Satan was truly beautiful, but his beauty was still only a faint reflection of the overwhelming beauty and glory of God. How ridiculous of Satan to think that he could become more beautiful than the God who had created him. Obviously, Satan had become so drunk with his own pride that he had lost all reason. He now wanted all of God's glory.

1 | Who Is Satan?

5. *I WILL MAKE MYSELF LIKE THE MOST HIGH*

> Isaiah 14:13-14 (NIV)
> *13) You said in your heart, "I will ascend to heaven; I will raise my throne above the stars of God; I will sit enthroned on the mount of assembly on the utmost heights of the sacred mountain.*
> *14) I will ascend above the tops of the clouds; I WILL MAKE MYSELF LIKE THE MOST HIGH."*

What do you think that Satan meant when he said *"I will make myself like the Most High"*?

WAR This means War

Satan's last "I will" seems to be the most tragic of the five. He actually thought he could be like God. Satan must have realized that he was but a mere creation of the all-powerful God. He had to have known that he was no match for the God of all creation. Even in the drunkenness of his pride he must have understood God's overwhelming greatness. How then did Satan imagine in his wildest thoughts that he could be like God? God is the only Being in all of eternity who is responsible only to Himself. No one tells God what to do. He does what He pleases. Nevertheless, Satan insisted on being like God in that he too wanted to answer to no one but himself. He was determined to be his own god and have all other created beings worship him.

THE GREATEST TRAGEDY OF ALL ETERNITY

Somewhere before time began, a terrible tragedy took place. Satan, the most beautiful, the wisest, and the most powerful of all created beings turned against God. Thus, he started a war with God that he could not and will not win.

III. WHAT DID GOD DO ABOUT SATAN'S REBELLION?

As we have seen, Satan became full of pride and rebellious against God. He rejected the will of God and instead chose to do his own will. That horrible decision is the worst tragedy of all eternity. Satan, in his incredible arrogance had actually created a devastating new belief. That belief was this: "Independence from God is better than dependence upon God." Put another way, Satan's new belief said that a created being could be far more successful and happy by worshipping himself, rather than God!

Clearly this was a serious challenge to God and His authority. Therefore, God's response to Satan's horrendous rebellion was both swift and final.

Ezekiel 28:16b & 17b (NIV)
16b) ...So I drove you in disgrace from the mount of God, and I expelled you, O guardian cherub, from among the fiery stones.
17b) ...So I threw you to the earth; I made a spectacle of you before kings.

Isaiah 14:12 (NIV)
12) How you have fallen from heaven, O morning star, son of the dawn! You have been cast down to the earth, you who once laid low the nations!

SATAN WAS STRIPPED OF HIS AUTHORITY

As we can see from the verses from Ezekiel and Isaiah, Satan was stripped of his authority to act for God. According to Ezekiel 28:16b, how do we know this is true?

_____

_____

_____

Satan's rebellion left him *"in disgrace."* He was stripped of his rank as guardian cherub of the throne of God and removed from his powerful office as head administrator in God's government.

SATAN WAS EXPELLED FROM HEAVEN

God, in His Holiness, could not tolerate rebellion and evil in His Kingdom. Therefore, He had to drive Satan from heaven. According to Ezekiel 28:16b, how do we know that Satan was kicked out of heaven?

_____

_____

_____

Ezekiel 28:16b goes on to say that Satan was *"expelled...from among the fiery stones"* (heaven). When someone is expelled from school what happens to them?

_____

_____

_____

It must have been a terrible day in heaven when Satan and the fallen angels who followed him had to be forcibly removed from the love and beauty of heaven. Though Satan was God's greatest and most privileged creation, things would never be the same for him again.

SATAN WAS THROWN DOWN TO THE EARTH

The Bible teaches that he was not only expelled from heaven, but actually thrown to the earth. All of us have had the embarrassing and painful experience of falling to the ground. In Isaiah 14 we see that Satan did not merely fall to the earth, but was violently thrown there by a holy and angry God.

1 Who Is Satan?

Who Is Satan?

> Isaiah 14:12 (NIV)
> *12) How you have fallen from heaven, O morning star, son of the dawn! You have been cast down to the earth....*
>
> Ezekiel 28:17b (NIV)
> *17b) ...So I threw you to the earth....*

Study the above passages and write down all of the phrases that describe Satan's fall.

_____

_____

_____

The great battle between God's Kingdom and Satan's Kingdom started when Satan, due to his pride and rebellion, thought he could take over the very throne of God. That was a terrible mistake. God stripped him of his authority as God's administrator. He was kicked out of heaven and thrown to earth. Though the battle between Satan and God began in heaven, much of that battle is now being fought on the earth. That means that all of us are caught in the middle of this horrible spiritual war. And Satan, in all of his hatred and anger towards God, is not about to let us escape from his vicious attacks!

Satan's Attack On Mankind

2 Satan's Attack On Mankind

We learned in chapter one that a major war broke out in heaven between Satan and God. We also learned that God chose not to destroy him, but rather to throw Satan out of heaven and down to earth because of his rebellion. Satan was confused by his pride and warped by his evil and still believed that he could defeat God. Though it was clearly a war he could never win, Satan set out to counterattack God through man.

> ## IN THIS STUDY WE WILL LOOK AT SATAN'S ATTACK ON MANKIND, MAN'S DEFEAT, AND GOD'S JUDGMENT ON BOTH FOR THEIR REBELLION.

2 | Satan's Attack On Mankind

I. SATAN ATTACKS MANKIND

Compared to God's army of angels and to Satan, man is small. At first glance, the entire human race seems completely insignificant in the great war between God and Satan. In Psalm 8 King David talked about the apparent insignificance of man.

> Psalm 8:3-4 (TLB)
> *3) When I look up into the night skies and see the work of your fingers—the moon and the stars you have made—*
> *4) I cannot understand how you can bother with mere puny man, to pay any attention to him!*

Yet, in spite of what appears to be man's smallness, God has declared that the human race is very, very important. Satan realizes the importance of mankind, and has chosen to focus his main attack on it.

Why do you think Satan has focused his main attack on man?

_____

_____

_____

Satan's Attack On Mankind   2

A. WHY DID SATAN ATTACK MANKIND?

As we saw in the last chapter, when Satan rebelled against God he was thrown to earth. Earth became Satan's domain. Then God, in His infinite wisdom, created man and appointed him to rule the earth in Satan's place. God made it very clear how much authority He was giving to man, as we can see in Genesis 1.

> Genesis 1:28 (NIV)
> 28) And God blessed them and said to them, "Be fruitful and increase in number; fill the earth and subdue it. Rule over the fish of the sea and the birds of the air and over every living creature that moves on the ground."

How do we know from this passage that God created mankind to have delegated authority over the earth?

_____

_____

_____

Satan's Attack On Mankind

Satan's Attack On Mankind | 2

God gave man the responsibility and the power to tame and take charge of the earth. God was saying something truly amazing to man. If man would simply trust God and obey Him, then God would help him make the earth into a true paradise forever. God was giving to insignificant man the kingdom that Satan was claiming for himself. He wanted to make the point that even the weak and small could be great in His Kingdom if they remained obedient and dependent upon Him. Imagine how wonderful Adam and Eve must have felt knowing they would be in charge of the world. And imagine how infuriated Satan must have been knowing they were in charge of what he thought was his own. Therefore, Satan in an attempt to get back at God, chose to attack the human race.

B. HOW DID SATAN ATTACK?

When God made Adam and Eve the rulers of the earth He gave them tremendous freedom. He knew that if they relied on His great wisdom they would be able to make the wise decisions necessary to tame the earth. However, along with their freedom, God gave Adam and Eve one command that was designed to test their willingness to obey Him. The Bible explains this command in Genesis 2.

> Genesis 2:16-17 (NIV)
> *16) And the Lord God commanded the man, "You are free to eat from any tree in the garden;*
> *17) but you must not eat from the tree of the knowledge of good and evil, for when you eat of it you will surely die."*

Why do you think God gave Adam and Eve this command?

_____

_____

_____

God wanted Adam and Eve to recognize that He had given them the most powerful freedom of all. He gave them the freedom to choose between obedience and disobedience. It was a choice between God's will or doing their own will. Though God is Holy and all-powerful, He wanted the man and the woman to freely choose whether they would serve God or serve themselves.

As we discussed in Chapter 1, Satan was the wisest of all of God's created beings. In his evil wisdom, Satan seemed to understand that the free choice God was giving to Adam and Eve was a perfect opportunity to attack and destroy them. He was aware that the chances of Adam and Eve rejecting God in order to worship him were small. However, he also knew that they could be tempted to reject God if they thought they could somehow become like gods themselves. It was obvious to Satan that this puny little man could only maintain his rule of the earth through God's power. Satan correctly reasoned that once man rejected God, he could step in and remake the world into his own dark and evil kingdom. In Genesis 3, the Bible tells us how Satan used horrible lies and deceptions to tempt man to rebel against God.

Satan's Attack On Mankind | 2

> Genesis 3:1-5 (NIV)
>
> 1) Now the serpent was more crafty than any of the wild animals the Lord God had made. He said to the woman, "Did God really say, 'You must not eat from any tree in the garden'?"
>
> 2) The woman said to the serpent, "We may eat fruit from the trees in the garden,
>
> 3) but God did say, 'You must not eat fruit from the tree that is in the middle of the garden, and you must not touch it, or you will die.'"
>
> 4) "You will not surely die," the serpent said to the woman.
>
> 5) "For God knows that when you eat of it your eyes will be opened, and you will be like God, knowing good and evil."

According to verse 1, how does God describe the serpent (Satan)?

_____

_____

_____ Hypes the Sin - Downplays Consequences

What do you think the Bible means when it says *"the serpent was more crafty than any of the wild animals"*?

_____

_____

_____

2 | Satan's Attack On Mankind

Satan's Attack On Mankind 2

Satan somehow entered a creature that was called the serpent. Most of us imagine this as a frightening, evil looking creature. However, it is likely that this creature was actually beautiful and spoke to Adam and Eve in a way that was very appealing and persuasive.

What was Satan trying to accomplish when he said *"Did God really say, 'You must not eat from any tree in the garden'?"*

_____

_____

_____

Satan had devised a very subtle lie that made God appear like He did not love Eve and did not have her best interests in mind. He implied that God was keeping them from eating any of the garden's fruit instead of just the fruit from the one tree. His trick was to cast doubt on God's truthfulness and to make God look like the great killjoy in the sky.

According to verses 2 & 3 what does Eve's answer to Satan tell us?

_____

_____

_____

Eve's answer to Satan shows that she had understood God's command in Genesis 2:16-17.

According to verse 4, what was Satan's second lie to Eve?

_____

_____

_____

Satan directly called God a liar. God told Adam and Eve that if they ate of the tree they "would surely die." He did not simply say they would die, He said they would "surely" die (Genesis 2:16-17). God made the consequences of eating the fruit crystal clear; and that consequence was death. Satan's lie mocked God's truthfulness.

Looking at our world today, how would we know God's promise about the consequences of sin is true?

_____

_____

_____

Satan's Attack On Mankind | 2

SATAN'S BIGGEST LIE OF ALL

The deception and lies Satan used in verses 1-4 were really only the groundwork for the big lie in verse 5. This lie was designed to convince Eve that God was holding back something that would be good for Adam and her. It was an attack on the very goodness of God. Satan said to Eve:

GENESIS 3:5-7 (NIV)
5) "For God knows that when you eat of it your eyes will be opened, and you will be like God, knowing good and evil."
6) When the woman saw that the fruit of the tree was for food and pleasing to the eye, and also desirable for gaining wisdom, she took some and ate it. She also gave some to her husband, who was with her, and he ate it.
7) Then the eyes of both of them were opened, and they realized they were naked; so they sewed fig leaves together and made coverings for themselves.

In verse 5, what did Satan want Eve to believe when he told her that *"God knows that when you eat of it your eyes will be opened?"*

_____

_____

_____

2 | Satan's Attack On Mankind

Satan was implying that God knew something that Eve didn't; that somehow God was keeping her in the dark and that she could be much wiser if she ate the fruit. Satan also implied that when Eve's eyes were opened by eating the fruit, she would somehow be like God.

In what way would Eve become like God when she ate the fruit?

_____

_____

_____

Eve would be able to lead her life without having to be dependent upon God. In other words, she could be her own god and do what she wanted to do. She would be free to experience the pleasures of sin. However, she would also learn in a horrible way what God already knew about evil. She would soon discover that her sin had enslaved her, and that even with all of her new-found freedom she would not be able to escape from its painful consequences.

According to verse 6 what three reasons did Eve use to convince herself that she should eat the fruit?

_____

_____

_____

Satan's Attack On Mankind

Satan's Attack On Mankind

Why do you think these reasons were not good enough for her to eat the fruit?

_____

_____

_____

All of Eve's reasons were selfish. Each reason showed that she did not trust God to do what was best for her. They demonstrated her false belief that she could meet her own needs independent of God. However, God had made it very clear that He would not allow rebellion. Therefore, when Adam and Eve rebelled against God they had to pay a very big price.

II. GOD ANNOUNCES THE CONSEQUENCES OF REBELLION BOTH TO SATAN AND TO MANKIND.

A. SATAN PAYS A TERRIBLE PRICE FOR HIS REBELLION AGAINST GOD.

When Adam and Eve rebelled against God it looked as if Satan had won the battle for the heart of mankind. Satan was successful at getting man to turn away from God. This gave Satan the freedom he needed to keep man under his evil power. It is not hard to imagine that Satan was feeling proud and boastful at the thought of having defeated God in the battle for the human race. However, God cannot be defeated. Instead, He made it known that it was Satan who would be defeated once and for all.

Soon after Adam and Eve's rebellion against God, God announced His plan to destroy Satan forever. He spoke of One who would come to give God a great victory over Satan and his kingdom. God said in Genesis 3:15,

> Genesis 3:15 (NIV)
> 15) "And I will put enmity between you and the woman, and between your offspring and hers; he will crush your head, and you will strike his heel."

A closer look at this verse shows us that God is predicting the coming of His Son, Jesus Christ, who would be born of a woman. God's message to Satan was not to be mistaken. Jesus Christ, the man, would come and totally defeat him. God went on to predict that there would be a terrible battle.

2 | Satan's Attack On Mankind

In Genesis 3:15 God said to Satan, *"And you will strike his **heel**."* What do you think *"and strike his **heel**"* means?

_____

_____

_____

While there is some mystery in this statement, we know that Christ was humiliated, severely beaten, and suffered a horrible death on the cross. He was "wounded for our transgressions, he was bruised for our iniquities" (Isaiah 53:5 KJV). Yet, because of the resurrection, Christ was merely wounded and not defeated. He returned to life as a victorious King.

God also said *"he will crush your* (Satan's) ***head**."* What do you think this means?

_____

_____

_____

When Jesus died on the cross Satan must have gleefully thought he had defeated God. However, when Jesus rose from the dead three days later it became apparent throughout all of Satan's evil kingdom that they had celebrated too soon (Revelation 20:10). No doubt Satan finally understood that the death of Jesus meant his ultimate defeat but a new life in Christ for mankind.

B. THE HUMAN RACE PAYS A TERRIBLE PRICE FOR THEIR REBELLION AGAINST GOD.

Satan was not the only one who had to suffer consequences for his rebellion. Adam and Eve also had a serious price to pay for their sins against God. They soon learned that there are always negative consequences for disobedience and rebellion against God. These consequences are listed beginning in Genesis 3:16.

> Genesis 3:16-19 (NIV)
>
> *16) To the woman he said, "I will greatly increase your pains in childbearing; with pain you will give birth to children. Your desire will be for your husband, and he will rule over you."* Frustrate the fire out of you
>
> *17) To Adam he said, "Because you listened to your wife and ate from the tree about which I commanded you, 'You must not eat of it,' "Cursed is the ground because of you; through painful toil you will eat of it, all the days of your life.*
>
> *18) It will produce thorns and thistles for you, and you will eat the plants of the field.*
>
> *19) By the sweat of your brow you will eat your food until you return to the ground, since from it you were taken; for dust you are and to dust you will return."*

Look at verse 16 and list the awful consequences for the woman.

_____

_____

_____

Look at verses 17-19 and list the awful consequences listed for the man.

_____

_____

_____

While there is some debate about the exact meaning of some of these consequences, it is certain that none of them were pleasant. God told Adam and Eve that their lives would be short and hard and then they would die. What an incredible turnaround! Just moments before they had the hope of spending eternity with God and having all of their needs supplied. Unfortunately, due to their own rebellion, they became the first human casualties in the great spiritual war that continues to devastate the human race.

Gen 3:15

CONCLUSION

Satan successfully deceived Eve. She believed his lies and allowed herself to be tricked into disobeying God. Her husband, Adam, was not fooled by Satan's lies. However, he still chose to disobey God. By eating the fruit he also bought into Satan's awful lie that he could be his own god. The consequences of their sin have been felt by every person who has ever lived. We are all born as slaves to sin and to Satan's lies. Our sin of rebellion has blinded us to both the truth about God and the truth about our own horrible condition. We have tried to be our own gods and have failed miserably. The Apostle Paul describes our terrible situation in Romans 6.

Romans 6:23 (NIV)
23) For the wages of sin is death, but the gift of God is eternal life in Christ Jesus our Lord.

NOTES

Jesus Defeats Satan Through His Life

3 Jesus Defeats Satan Through His Life

INTRODUCTION

Satan must have been thrilled at knowing that he had helped to turn man away from God. He was successful at getting Adam and Eve and all of mankind to believe his twisted and evil philosophy. That philosophy is this: "Independence from God is life and dependence upon God is death; to be happy you must be your own god." He must also have been very pleased that he was now the "prince of this world." Yet, deep in Satan's heart God's promise to destroy him no doubt made him uneasy (Genesis 3:15). If it didn't, it should have because God always keeps His promises. Two thousand years ago God did keep His promise by sending a mighty warrior into battle against Satan. Who would ever have thought that this mighty warrior would turn out to be none other than God, Himself, who became a man in the humble person of Jesus Christ.

> ## IN THIS STUDY WE WILL SEE HOW THE MIGHTY WARRIOR, JESUS CHRIST, DEFEATED SATAN'S LIES THROUGH HIS LIFE.

3 | Jesus Defeats Satan Through His Life

I. GOD SHATTERED SATAN AND HIS LIES THROUGH CHRIST'S DEPENDENCE UPON THE FATHER.

The Bible teaches that Jesus Christ is the most unique person that ever lived; unique in that He is both completely God and completely man. These two natures remain forever separate, but form one person, the perfect God-Man, Jesus Christ.

This Jesus Christ had to have been the most powerful, yet baffling enemy Satan had ever faced. Powerful, because He was God and baffling because He was a simple Jewish peasant who was human in every way. By coming to the earth as a man, Jesus Christ was able to model to the rest of mankind what it meant to be totally dependent upon God. The Bible talks about this in Philippians 2.

> PHILIPPIANS 2:6-7 (NCV)
> *6) Christ himself was like God in everything. He was equal with God. But he did not think that being equal with God was something to be held on to.*
> *7) He gave up his place with God and made himself nothing. He was born to be a man and became like a servant.*

Jesus Defeats Satan Through His Life

3

What do you think the Bible means when it says *"He gave up His place with God and made Himself nothing"*?

_____

_____

_____

Jesus Christ came to earth as both God and man. Because He was God, He possessed all the powers of God. Yet, most of the time, He chose not to use these powers. Instead, He chose to temporarily lay them aside and walk as a man in total dependence upon the Father.

Therefore, when Christ *"made Himself nothing"*, He set an important example for us. He wanted us to learn that real living comes from total dependence upon God and complete obedience to Him. He very clearly summed up his goal for life when He spoke to his disciples in John 4:34.

JOHN 4:34 (NIV)
34) "My food," said Jesus, "is to do the will of Him who sent me and to finish His work. "

Jesus Defeats Satan Through His Life

When Jesus said *"My food is to do the will of Him who sent me,"* what did He mean by the words *"my food"*?

_____

_____

_____

When Jesus spoke those words, He had been so busy helping others that He had not taken the time to eat all day long. The disciples, knowing how hungry he must have been, urged Him to eat something. Jesus's response was dramatic. He made it clear that His food, so to speak, His energy to meet life's challenges came from doing God's will and obeying Him in all things. He was teaching His disciples that depending upon God was the only way to truly have your needs met. In fact, in John 14, Jesus told His disciples that His total dependence upon God gave Him a great advantage.

> JOHN 14:30-31 (NIV)
> *30) I will not speak with you much longer, for the prince of this world is coming. He has no hold on me,*
> *31) but the world must learn that I love the Father and that I do exactly what my Father has commanded me....*

Jesus Defeats Satan Through His Life

According to verse 30, what did Jesus mean when He said Satan had *"no hold on me"*?

_____

_____

_____

Christ knew that He was coming to the end of His life. He knew that Satan was about to launch a furious attack designed to completely destroy Him. Despite this, Satan could neither make Him afraid nor cause Him to change His mind. Because Christ's mind was so in-tune with the Father, Satan's empty lies and deceitful philosophies had no hold on him.

Satan must have been furious when he discovered that Christ had such dependance upon His Father. Nevertheless, Satan continued his attacks. He would use his most powerful temptations in his attempt to defeat Christ.

II. GOD SHATTERED SATAN AND HIS LIES WHEN CHRIST RESISTED TEMPTATION

Jesus Christ made a powerful statement when He said in John 14:30 *"he has no hold on me"*. Satan must have been infuriated when, as Christ was facing His death, He was still able to say *"he has no hold on me"*. Satan, the father of lies, knew that Jesus was telling the truth. Throughout Christ's life, Satan worked hard to lure Him into giving in to temptation. The Bible does not give us every temptation faced by Christ. Scripture does, however, give us a detailed picture of a classic encounter between the great tempter, Satan, and Jesus Christ. In this encounter, we will see that Satan tempted Jesus in three ways. Let's call these temptations "the great confrontation in the desert."

A. THE FIRST TEMPTATION - SATAN TEMPTS JESUS TO MEET HIS NEEDS APART FROM GOD.

MATTHEW 4:1-4 (NIV)
1) Then Jesus was led by the Spirit into the desert to be tempted by the devil.
2) After fasting forty days and forty nights, He was hungry.
3) The tempter came to Him and said, "If you are the Son of God, tell these stones to become bread."
4) Jesus answered, "It is written: 'Man does not live on bread alone, but on every word that comes from the mouth of God.'"

Jesus Defeats Satan Through His Life

As verse 2 tells us, Jesus had not eaten for forty days and forty nights. He was so hungry that His desire to eat was a greater physical need than most of us have ever experienced. In verse 3 Satan tempted Jesus to meet this tremendous need. He said, *"If you are the Son of God tell these stones to become bread."*

Why do you think it would have been wrong for Jesus to turn the stone into bread?

_____

_____

_____

On first thought, turning stones into bread seemed like a reasonable thing for Jesus to do. After all, He had a great need and because He is the Son of God, He had the power to meet that need. However, when we understand what Satan was really asking Jesus to do we can see what a horrible temptation it was. Satan wanted Jesus to ignore God's promise that He would meet all of His needs. He was tempting Jesus to act independently of God and instead, be dependent upon himself. However, as we can see in verse 4, Jesus was not fooled by Satan's deception.

> MATTHEW 4:4 (NIV)
> *4) Jesus answered, "It is written: 'Man does not live on bread alone, but on every word that comes from the mouth of God.'"*

What do you think Jesus means when he said, *"man can not live by bread alone"*?

_____

_____

_____

Jesus quoted a verse to Satan from the Old Testament (Deuteronomy 8:3). This verse is a lesson learned by the children of Israel who wandered in the desert for forty years. Each day God provided them with special food (manna) so they could survive. God, in His love and power, was seeking to teach them to depend on Him to meet even their most basic needs. Jesus knew that Satan was tempting Him to meet His own needs without depending upon God. Jesus resisted this temptation and clearly declared to Satan that He had no intention of acting independently of God. He was committed to remaining dependent upon God for all of His needs, no matter how great they might be.

B. THE SECOND TEMPTATION - SATAN DARES JESUS TO TEMPT GOD.

MATTHEW 4:5-7 (NIV)
5) Then the devil took Him to the holy city and had Him stand on the highest point of the temple.
6) "If you are the Son of God," he said, "throw yourself down. For it is written: "'He will command His angels concerning you, and they will lift you up in their hands, so that you will not strike your foot against a stone.'"
7) Jesus answered him, "It is also written: 'Do not put the Lord your God to the test.'"

As we can see from verse 5, Satan put Christ into a dramatic situation. He led Him to the very peak of the temple in Jerusalem which overlooked the Kidron Valley nearly 500 feet below. This was a huge drop. It would be like standing atop a 50-story building. It was a long way down. From this frightening height Satan said to Jesus -

---

MATTHEW 4:6 (NIV)
6) "If you are the Son of God," he said, "throw yourself down. For it is written: "'He will command His angels concerning You, and they will lift You up in their hands, so that You will not strike your foot against a stone.'"

---

3 Jesus Defeats Satan Through His Life

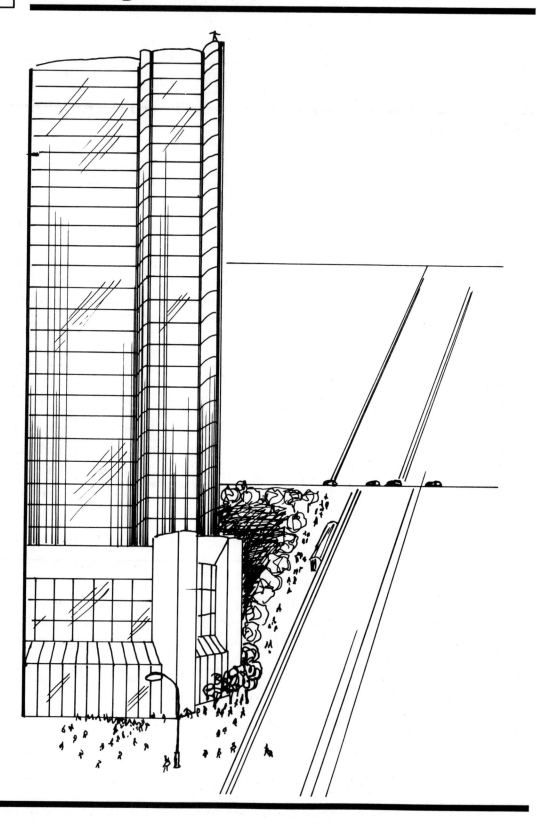

Jesus Defeats Satan Through His Life

Satan, the great deceiver, was now using Scripture, itself, to tempt Jesus to sin. In essence, Satan said to Jesus, "If you want to live by the Scripture then live by this one," and he quoted Psalm 91:11-12.

Why do you think it would have been wrong for Jesus to throw Himself down from the top of the temple?

_____

_____

_____

Satan was attempting to manipulate and trick Jesus by quoting this Scripture out of context. That is to say, he took this one passage and did not include other Scriptures on the same subject. In essence, he was saying, "Since you say you are the Son of God, and since Scripture promises that God will protect you, why don't you go ahead and jump? Why don't you prove it?" Satan wanted Christ to accept a dare in order to prove that He was the Son of God, and that God would indeed protect Him.

Jesus, however, refused to accept this treacherous dare. He knew that Satan had quoted the Scripture out of context and twisted its meaning. Jesus realized that Satan was trying to trick Him into testing God. Therefore, Christ responded with another verse, this one from Deuteronomy 6:16:

> MATTHEW 4:7 (NIV)
> *7) Jesus answered him, "It is also written: 'Do not put the Lord your God to the test.'"*

3 | Jesus Defeats Satan Through His Life

What do you think it means to test God?

_____

_____

_____

We are guilty of testing God when we expect Him to answer our demands even though our motives are selfish and insincere. God views this kind of action as deliberate sin. For example:

-**We may be testing God when we rush into a dangerous, but avoidable situation and then expect to be rescued.**
-**We may be testing God if we are desperately ill, and instead of seeking a doctor's care, we blindly believe that God, alone, will heal us.**
-**We may be testing God when we spend money we don't have assuming God will somehow provide.**
-**We test God when we knowingly get into sin, but expect God to forgive us without consequences.** _Don't push your Grace._

Taking God's promises out of context is testing Him and is a serious crime! King David talked about this in Psalm 19.

> PSALM 19:13 (TLB)
> 13) _And keep me from deliberate wrongs; help me to stop doing them. Only then can I be free of guilt and innocent of some great crime._

Jesus in His purity and wisdom refused to accept Satan's dare to test God. He refused to jump off of the temple peak and presume upon God's promise to protect Him. We need to be careful not to fall into Satan's trap by testing God.

66

C. THE THIRD TEMPTATION - SATAN OFFERS JESUS ALL HE HAS FOR ONE ACT OF WORSHIP.

No doubt, Satan was getting progressively more frustrated and angry. He must have felt that his first two temptations of Jesus would certainly cause Him to fall. However, as we will see from Matthew 4:8-11 he was sadly mistaken.

MATTHEW 4:8-11 (NIV)
8) Again, the devil took Him to a very high mountain and showed Him all the kingdoms of the world and their splendor.
9) "All this I will give you," he said, "if You will bow down and worship me."
10) Jesus said to him, "Away from me, Satan! For it is written: 'Worship the Lord your God, and serve Him only.'". Just One - Do it once
11) Then the devil left Him, and angels came and attended Him. 33%

From Matthew 4:8, describe in your own words what you think Jesus saw.

_____

_____

_____

It is probable that Jesus saw in one view all of the world's kingdoms, whether past, present or future. In addition, He saw the incredible wealth and power of those kingdoms. This overwhelming display might have been the greatest ever seen outside of Heaven itself. Having put on this tremendous show, Satan then made his very best offer to Jesus.

> MATTHEW 4:9 (NIV)
> *9) "All this I will give you," he said, "if You will bow down and worship me."*

As we have seen, Satan knew the Scripture well. It is almost certain that he knew Psalm 2, in which God had already promised Christ all the Kingdoms of the World...

> PSALMS 2:7-8 (NIV)
> *7) I will proclaim the decree of the Lord: He said to me, "You are my Son; today I have become your Father.*
> *8) Ask of me, and I will make the nations your inheritance, the ends of the earth your possession.*

Jesus Defeats Satan Through His Life

However, it is also very likely that Satan knew the price Christ would have to pay before these Kingdoms would be His. Psalm 22 and Isaiah 53 both speak of Christ first having to die on the cross. Thus, Satan's offer of these Kingdoms was actually a treacherous lie. In reality he was offering Jesus his kingship without having to suffer the horrible death of crucifixion. In other words, Satan offered the goods without talking about the cost. This is always Satan's biggest and most dangerous deception.

Satan, in his evil delusion, believed that he could do to Christ what he had done to Adam and Eve. He believed that if he could just get Christ to fall into sin, He would lose his power and therefore, fall under Satan's authority. Satan implied that Jesus could gain all of the kingdoms of the world for one simple bow at his feet. But, in truth, as just one bite of the forbidden fruit caused the death of mankind, so just one simple bow to Satan would have caused the downfall of Christ Himself. The only thing Satan was really offering to Jesus was bondage and death.

Satan's ultimate goal is made clear in this passage. He wanted to be worshipped. He is addicted to it! He craves it! Why? Because he has always craved to be God. However, his cravings will never be met. He is the great pretender. Therefore, Jesus's answer to Satan was both swift and powerful.

MATTHEW 4:10 (NIV)
10) Jesus said to him, "Away from me, Satan! For it is written: 'Worship the Lord your God, and serve Him only.'"

Jesus Defeats Satan Through His Life

3 Jesus Defeats Satan Through His Life

What do you think Jesus meant when He said *"away from me, Satan!"*?

_____

_____

_____

Jesus was declaring that even though Satan had taken his best shots, it would have no effect on Him. Jesus, a holy man, was no doubt sickened by all the lies and evil that were laid before Him. Finally, in the power of God, He ordered Satan to leave. However, before Satan left, Jesus forced him to listen to a great Bible truth that must have both angered and terrified him.

> DEUTERONOMY 6:13
> *"Worship the Lord your God, and serve Him only."*

Jesus knew that who we worship is who we will serve. Jesus was declaring the truth that, **Dependence upon God is Life and that Independence of God is Death.** Or as Matthew put it:

> MATTHEW 16:26 (NASV)
> *26) "For what will a man be profited, if he gains the whole world, and forfeits his soul? Or what will a man give in exchange for his soul?*

Jesus Defeats Satan Through His Life

CONCLUSION

Satan did everything in his power to tempt Christ to sin. It was Satan's goal to fool Jesus into depending on himself rather than trusting God. Satan's ultimate ambition was simple. He craved for Jesus to worship him. But, Satan met more than his match in Jesus Christ. He encountered someone who would not only refuse to fall for his lies, but would ultimately destroy him at the mighty battle on the Cross!

4 Jesus Defeats Satan Through His Death

SATAN'S POWER OVER MANKIND

4 Jesus Defeats Satan Through His Death

As we saw in the last chapter Jesus Christ was God in the flesh. He came to do battle with Satan, and was committed to exposing both Satan's lies and his philosophy, and to destroying his power over mankind. The Bible says in I John 3:8,

---

I JOHN 3:8c (NCV)
8c) "The Son of God came for this purpose: to destroy the devil's work."

Scripture is clear that Christ did not come to simply harass Satan, or slow him down, but to completely destroy him. Satan for his part was determined to furiously oppose this mighty warrior—Jesus Christ. From the time of Christ's birth to the moment on the cross when He said "It is finished," Satan did all in his power to bring about His downfall. He was determined to bring Christ under his dominion at any cost. Nevertheless, he was doomed to fail. Satan and his demonic forces must have been incredibly frustrated by Christ's total dependence upon the Father. They could not tempt Him to sin no matter what they tried. He was absolutely committed to obeying His heavenly Father, no matter what the price.

It must have finally become apparent that the only way to stop Jesus would be to kill Him. Little did Satan know that as he made his devious schemes to destroy Jesus, he was actually planning his own destruction.

4 | Jesus Defeats Satan Through His Death

> ## IN THIS CHAPTER WE WILL DISCUSS HOW SATAN'S ATTEMPTS TO KILL JESUS ONLY LEAD TO HIS OWN DEFEAT.

I. SATAN'S PLAN TO KILL JESUS INVOLVED MANY PEOPLE.

As has already been stated, Satan longed to see Christ come under his domain. At first his strategy seemed to be one of tempting Christ to worship him and avoid death by skipping the cross. However, when Christ resisted all of Satan's temptations, he had to change his strategy. Satan decided to use all of his mighty forces to kill Christ. These forces included many people who had chosen not to believe in Him. As the planned day for Christ's destruction on the cross grew closer, Satan's personal involvement in this horrible plan grew more clear.

Jesus Defeats Satan Through His Death

SATAN AND JUDAS

The last week of Christ's life was a time of intense spiritual warfare between God and the forces of evil. The Bible tells us in Luke that in the Upper Room, Satan took direct control of his plan to kill Jesus.

LUKE 22:3-4 (TLB)
3) Then Satan entered in Judas Iscariot, who was one of the twelve disciples,
4) and he went over to the chief priests and captains of the Temple guards to discuss the best way to betray Jesus to them.

Why do you think Satan decided to enter Judas?

_____

_____

_____

While it is almost unthinkable that one of Jesus' own disciples actually betrayed Him, clearly Judas must be held responsible for his actions. However, it may have been that this deed was so horrible that Satan had to empower him to make sure the betrayal would be accomplished.

Jesus Defeats Satan Through His Death

SATAN AND THE RELIGIOUS LEADERS

As Christ headed toward the cross He announced that it was Satan who was in control of the horrible events that were unfolding. When Christ came out of the garden He used very strong words to confront those who had come to arrest Him.

LUKE 22:52b-53 (NCV)
52b) Jesus said to them, "Why did you come out here with swords and sticks? Do you think I am a criminal?
53) I was with you every day in the Temple. Why didn't you try to arrest me there? But this is your time—the time when darkness rules."

What do you think Christ meant when He said *"But this is your time—the time when darkness rules"*?

_____

_____

_____

In the trial and crucifixion of Jesus we are shown a glimpse of just how horrible Satan and his followers can be. The lies, beatings, mockery and the horrible death on the cross all demonstrated Satan's total rebellion and hatred of God. The power of that hatred was so great that it would be satisfied with nothing less than the death of Christ. In all of history, this may have been the greatest force of evil ever brought together in a battle against God.

II. SATAN'S ALL-OUT PUSH FOR VICTORY WAS TURNED INTO HIS TOTAL DEFEAT.

When Christ finally died on the cross, Satan, no doubt, felt that he had stopped God's attack on his kingdom. Little did he know that God had allowed this vicious assault upon Christ. Satan, in his all-out attack to destroy Christ, helped bring about his own horrible defeat. The Bible talks about this in I Corinthians 2.

I CORINTHIANS 2:7-8 (NIV)
7) No, we speak of God's secret wisdom, a wisdom that has been hidden and that God destined for our glory before time began.
8) None of the rulers of this age understood it, for if they had, they would not have crucified the Lord of glory.

What do you think God's secret wisdom is?

_____

_____

_____

4 Jesus Defeats Satan Through His Death

Jesus Defeats Satan Through His Death

When the Bible refers to God's secret wisdom it is talking about the gospel. In other words, through Christ's death and resurrection those who put their faith in Christ will be rescued from Satan's evil kingdom and be given eternal life with God.

Who are *"the rulers of this age"*?

_____

_____

_____

"The rulers of this age" refer not only to the human rulers who put Christ to death, but also Satan and his demonic forces who are behind the earthly rulers.

Why do you think the Bible says *"the rulers of this age would not have crucified the Lord of Glory"* if they had really understood God's plan?

_____

_____

_____

4 | Jesus Defeats Satan Through His Death

Satan and his demonic forces would never have planned their own defeat. They clearly did not understand that Christ's death and resurrection would be God's way of forgiving man for his sins, and rescuing him from Satan's Kingdom. In fact, it is quite possible that when Christ rose from the dead, the most surprised person of all was Satan, himself. His goal had been to destroy Christ's ministry. Instead, he was shocked when he discovered that the tortured and broken person he helped to nail to the cross had become a mighty foe who had conquered death itself. Resurrection Day must have been a terrible day in Satan's Kingdom. Surely the truth found in I John 3:8 must have at last become a horrible reality to Satan.

I JOHN 3:8c (NCV)
8c) "The Son of God came for this purpose: to destroy the devil's work."

III. SATAN AND HIS ARMY WERE UTTERLY HUMILIATED AT THE CROSS AND MANKIND WAS FREED FROM THE FEAR OF DEATH.

A. AT THE CROSS JESUS HUMILIATED SATAN AND HIS FORCES.

As we have mentioned, when Christ hung on the cross, Satan and his demonic forces went all-out to destroy Him. They, no doubt, were belittling him and waiting eagerly and with delight for him to die. But, in one great motion, God threw them aside as Christ became the victorious winner and they became the defeated and humiliated foe. Put another way, when Jesus said "It is finished"—**they were finished**. The Apostle Paul tells us about Satan's defeat and the humiliation of his army in Colossians 2:15.

Colossians 2:15 (NIV)
15) And having disarmed the powers and authorities, he made a public spectacle of them, triumphing over them by the cross.

---

4 Jesus Defeats Satan Through His Death

Jesus Defeats Satan Through His Death

What does the Bible mean when it says that Christ *"disarmed the powers and authorities"*?

_____

_____

_____

The word *"disarmed"* basically means to unclothe or to strip naked. Satan had clothed himself with lies. He actually had the world believing that dependence upon God was death and independence from God was life. At the cross Jesus completely exposed this lie by his total obedience and dependence upon the Father. His dependence was so great that He gave his life in a cruel and painful death. God, however, rewarded Christ for his dependence. Christ became a conqueror who will be worshipped by all creation for ever! (Philippians 2:9-11).

According to Colossians 2:15 Christ also made a *"public spectacle"* of Satan and his army. What do you think this means?

_____

_____

_____

4 | Jesus Defeats Satan Through His Death

Jesus Defeats Satan Through His Death | 4

In Christ's day the Roman army was an unbeatable force. Each time they defeated an enemy, they would bring the best and the strongest of the captured soldiers back to Rome. Then they would hold a huge parade led by the conquering general. The captured soldiers would be chained to the general's chariot so that all of Rome could see how total and complete the defeat of the army had been.

The Bible says that Christ made a *"public spectacle"* of Satan and his army much the way the great Roman armies did with their defeated enemies. Satan had deceived the world into believing that he and his forces were all powerful and undefeatable. Mankind had come under his power due to sin. But when Christ died on the cross He broke Satan's power over mankind and took Satan and his forces captive. His victory was complete. As Paul tells us in the last phrase of Colossians 2:15—*"triumphing over them by the cross"*. Mankind was no longer imprisoned by the power of Satan. He now had an opportunity to escape from Satan's bondage and lies. He was now free to turn to a conqueror who was full of power and truth—the mighty warrior, Jesus Christ.

B. AT THE CROSS JESUS DESTROYED THE FEAR OF DEATH WHICH SATAN HAD USED TO ENSLAVE MANKIND.

Until the crucifixion of Jesus, Satan had real power over mankind. It was as though man was a slave to Satan, and could find no way out of this bondage. Perhaps the most horrible part of his power over mankind was his ability to stir up the terror of death in them. However, by His death, Jesus broke the power of this terrible fear. In Hebrews 2:14-15, the Bible talks about Christ's destruction of Satan's hold.

HEBREWS 2:14-15 (NIV)
14) Since the children have flesh and blood, he too shared in their humanity so that by his death he might destroy him who holds the power of death—that is, the devil—
15) and free those who all their lives were held in slavery by their fear of death.

According to Hebrews 2:14 the Bible says that by Christ's death, He destroyed Satan. What do you think the Bible means when it says He destroyed Satan?

_____

_____

_____

Jesus Defeats Satan Through His Death

When the Bible talks about destroying Satan, it does not mean that somehow the devil has been killed or ceases to exist. It is obvious that for the moment he is alive and very active. However, what Christ accomplished was to take his power and make it completely ineffective against those who trust Christ. Therefore, Satan is now just a shadow of what he once was. He and his mighty army were stripped of their power.

The Bible says that Christ destroyed *"Him (Satan) who holds the power of death."* What do you think Satan's *"power of death"* is?

_____

_____

_____

Satan is the great destroyer who hates mankind. It was his intent that all men should be put to death, both physically and spiritually (John 8:44). When man sinned against God, however, it was God, not Satan, who pronounced the death penalty. Yet Satan, using God's decree of death, taunted mankind about the hopelessness of his future.

The Bible says in Hebrews 2:15 that Christ's death freed *"those who all their lives were held in slavery by their fear of death."* How do you think Christ's death made man free from the fear of death?

_____

_____

_____

4 Jesus Defeats Satan Through His Death

Death was the weapon Satan used against mankind. However, Jesus, through his death, used Satan's own weapon against him. When Jesus died on the cross he paid the penalty of death which God had decreed for all mankind. Every person who trusts Christ is now guaranteed eternal life, and therefore needs no longer fear mere physical death. Jesus pulled the weapon of death out of Satan's hands and forever broke it's power to create fear in the hearts of Christians.

CONCLUSION

While hanging on the cross, Jesus said, "It is finished". That is, in a powerful and perfect way Jesus accomplished what He set out to do. He came to destroy the works of Satan and to set men free from their sin. At the cross, Jesus did it all. He exposed Satan's philosophy as a lie. He shattered Satan's power to enslave mankind by their fear of death. And he turned Satan into a powerless enemy for all who trust Christ as Savior.

Satan's Attack On Christians

5 | Satan's Attack On Christians

INTRODUCTION

In Chapter 4 we saw that Satan and his army were defeated by Christ at the cross. But that does not mean that Satan is powerless. He is still alive and in his destructive hate he wants to destroy Christians more than ever before. Though his attacks are devious and vicious, we must never forget the good news of the Cross. Satan's power has been made useless against every Christian who by faith stands with Christ.

> ## IN THIS DISCUSSION WE WILL SEEK TO UNDERSTAND WHY SATAN HATES CHRISTIANS AND LEARN SOME OF HIS DESTRUCTIVE PLANS TO DEFEAT THEM.

5 | Satan's Attack On Christians

I. WHY DOES SATAN HATE CHRISTIANS?

A. SATAN HATES CHRISTIANS BECAUSE THEY HAVE BEEN RESCUED BY GOD.

Satan must have been shocked when Christ rose from the dead. He must have begun to understand that his plan to kill Christ and stop His ministry could not work. He must also have been horrified when he saw that many of Christ's disciples had been transformed from grieving and fearful doubters to dedicated and fearless Christians. It must have become increasingly clear to Satan that there was an army of people who would resist both his deceitful lies and his destructive schemes. Satan was at last realizing what the book of First Peter tells us about this new army of Christians.

> I PETER 2:9 (NIV)
> *9) But you are a chosen people, a royal priesthood, a holy nation, a people belonging to God, that you may declare the praises of him who called you out of darkness into his wonderful light.*

Satan's Attack On Christians

According to First Peter 2:9 how are Christians described?

_____

_____

_____

According to First Peter 2:9 what does the Bible mean when it says Christians have been called *"out of darkness into his wonderful light"*?

_____

_____

_____

Satan was under the false belief that somehow he could keep mankind trapped in his lies, confusion and darkness. However, Jesus Himself made it clear how wrong Satan was when he announced in John 8 that everyone who followed him would be forever free of that darkness.

JOHN 8:12 (NIV)
12) *"...I am the light of the world. Whoever follows me will never walk in darkness, but will have the light of life."*

B. SATAN HATES CHRISTIANS BECAUSE THEY REFUSE TO BELIEVE HIS LIES.

As we have seen throughout this manual, Satan's main philosophy is this: "Dependence upon God is death and independence from God is life. Therefore, in order to be truly happy, one needs to be his own god." However, those who trust Christ as their Savior live a life that is in total disagreement with Satan's lie. Christians believe that by trusting in Christ and Christ alone they can find real joy and purpose in life. Jesus, Himself, taught this basic truth.

JOHN 15:5 (TLB)
5) "Yes, I am the Vine; you are the branches, Whoever lives in me and I in him shall produce a large crop of fruit. For apart from me you can't do a thing."

What does John 15:5 mean when it says *"apart from me you can't do a thing"*?

_____

_____

_____

5 | Satan's Attack On Christians

Christ did not mean that we could not do any kind of activity apart from Him. He was saying that any activity we do without Him is a waste of our time, is destructive and ultimately leads to spiritual death.

It is God's intention that all Christians have this kind of dependence upon and devotion to Him. Obviously, Satan hates Christians who are committed to God instead of his own destructive philosophy. He wants to keep every Christian from being dependent upon God. The Bible talks about Satan's destructive plan for Christians in II Corinthians.

> II CORINTHIANS 11:3 (TLB)
> 3) But I am frightened, fearing that in some way you will be led away from your pure and simple devotion to our Lord, just as Eve was deceived by Satan in the Garden of Eden.

What do you think *"pure and simple devotion to our Lord"* means?

_____

_____

_____

Satan's Attack On Christians

C. SATAN HATES CHRISTIANS BECAUSE THEY ARE ABLE TO ROB HIS KINGDOM BY BRINGING OTHERS TO CHRIST.

The Bible teaches that Jesus not only wants man to be totally dependent upon Him, but also to obey His commands. One of Christ's greatest commands to his followers was to go out and tell others about Him so that they might be rescued from Satan's kingdom of darkness. Jesus said in Mark 16:15,

> MARK 16:15 (NIV)
> *15) He said to them, "Go into all the world and preach the good news to all creation.*

Christians who obey this command of Christ are a direct threat to Satan. He wants to keep as many people as possible fooled by his lies and enslaved in his kingdom. The Bible talks about this in II Corinthians 4.

> II CORINTHIANS 4:3-4 (NCV)
> *3) The Good News that we preach may be hidden. But it is hidden only to those who are lost.*
> *4) The devil who rules this world has blinded the minds of those who do not believe.*
> *They cannot see the light of the Good News—the Good News about the glory of Christ, who is exactly like God.*

Satan's Attack On Christians

According to II Corinthians 4:3 what is *"the good news that we preach"*?

_____

_____

_____

According to verse 4 what is Satan trying to do to keep people from believing the Good News?

_____

_____

_____

God has decided to use Christians as His spokesman to tell others about Christ. Satan knows this. He knows that if he can stop Christians from telling non-Christians about Christ he can keep them in his trap. Therefore, he furiously battles to stop Christians from sharing their faith. Thus, we can begin to understand what the Bible says about Satan in I Peter 5.

I PETER 5:8 (TLB)
8) Be careful—watch out for attacks from Satan, your great enemy. He prowls around like a hungry, roaring lion, looking for some victim to tear apart.

Satan's Attack On Christians

II. SATAN USES THE WORLD TO LURE CHRISTIANS AWAY FROM DEPENDENCE UPON GOD!

Christians, who are in a minority, are surrounded by people who are in Satan's kingdom and are fooled into believing his lies. These people with their false beliefs and false values are part of what the Bible calls **"The World."** The World is all of the false attitudes and actions designed by Satan and believed by those in Satan's kingdom. These beliefs and attitudes are rebellious towards God and are designed to turn men away from God. The Bible describes "The World" in I John 2.

I JOHN 2:15-17 (NASV)
15) Do not love the world, nor the things in the world. If any one loves the world, the love of the Father is not in him.
16) For all that is in the world, the lust of the flesh and the lust of the eyes and the boastful pride of life, is not from the Father, but is from the world.
17) And the world is passing away, and also its lusts; but the one who does the will of God abides forever.

Satan's Attack On Christians

According to verse 16 there are three ways in which the World attacks mankind and draws Christians away from God. What are they?

_____

_____

_____

THE LUST OF THE FLESH

What do you think *"the lust of the flesh"* is?

_____

_____

_____

Satan's Attack On Christians

The *"lust of the flesh"* is a belief or attitude that attempts to convince us that the thrill of passion is far more important than seeking or depending upon God. Satan wants us to believe that satisfying our passions is an important part of finding personal fulfillment. For example, he wants us to believe:

> **-that thrilling our senses with the misuse of sex is far more important than seeking and knowing God.**
>
> **-that thrilling our senses with overeating (gluttony) is far more important than seeking or knowing God.**
>
> **-that thrilling our senses with the misuse of drugs or alcohol is far more important than seeking or knowing God.**
>
> **-that thrilling our senses by indulging in laziness is far more important than seeking or knowing God.**
>
> **-that thrilling our senses with partying is far more important than seeking or knowing God.**

The lies of lust of the flesh want us to believe that passion is a true god. These lies are an attempt to draw us away from seeking and depending upon God. These lies are summed up in Isaiah 22:13.

ISAIAH 22:13 (NCV)
13) But look. The people are happy. There are wild parties. They kill the cattle and the sheep. They eat the food and drink the wine. They say, "Let us eat and drink because tomorrow we will die."

Satan's Attack On Christians

THE LUST OF THE EYES

What do you think the *"lust of the eyes"* is?

_____

_____

_____

The *"lust of the eyes"* is a belief or attitude that attempts to convince us that the desire for possessions is far more important than seeking or depending upon God. Satan wants us to believe that satisfying our desire for possessions is an important part of finding personal fulfillment. For example he wants us to believe:

-**that getting positive self-esteem from owning things is far more important than seeking and knowing God.**
-**that working too many hours in order to buy possessions is far more important than seeking and knowing God.**
-**that owning the most stylish clothes is far more important than seeking and knowing God.**
-**that owning a car is far more important than seeking and knowing God.**

The lies of the lust of the eyes want us to believe that possessions are a true god. These lies are an attempt to draw us away from seeking and depending upon God. God warns us about believing these lies in I Timothy 6:10.

I TIMOTHY 6:10 (NCV)
10) The love of money causes all kinds of evil. Some people have left the true faith because they want to get more and more money. But they have caused themselves much sorrow.

Satan's Attack On Christians

Satan's Attack On Christians

THE BOASTFUL PRIDE OF LIFE

What do you think *"the boastful pride of life"* is?

_____

_____

_____

The *"boastful pride of life"* is the belief or attitude that attempts to convince us that the desire for power, position and fame is more important than seeking or depending upon God! Satan wants us to believe that satisfying our desire for these things is an important part of finding personal fulfillment. For example, he wants us to believe:

-that being popular with our peers is more important than
    seeking and knowing God.
-that having authority over other people is more important
    than seeking and knowing God.
-that being a well-known athlete is more important than
    seeking and knowing God.
-that just the right look in appearance, clothes and lifestyle is
    more important than seeking and knowing God.

Satan's Attack On Christians | 5

The lies of the boastful pride of life want us to believe that power, position, and fame are worth finding no matter what the cost. These lies are an attempt to draw us away from seeking and depending upon God. The Bible tells us about these lies in Psalm 39:6.

> PSALM 39:6 (NASV)
> 6) "Surely every man walks about as a phantom; Surely they make an uproar for nothing; He amasses riches, and does not know who will gather them.

Clearly, Satan hates Christians. He wants to attack them through the World. His hope is that the World's strong influence will lure the believer away from dependence upon God. This attack by Satan upon mankind is nothing less than a furious war against God. And anyone who believes the lies of the World sets himself up as an enemy of God. The Bible makes this very clear in James 4:4.

> JAMES 4:4 (NCV)
> 4) So, you people are not loyal to God! You should know that loving the world is the same as hating God. So if a person wants to be a friend of the world, he makes himself God's enemy.

III. SATAN USES THE FLESH TO LURE CHRISTIANS AWAY FROM DEPENDENCE UPON GOD!

Satan wages a furious war against the Christian from without through what the Bible calls the World—that is, non-Christians and their value system that is contrary to God. But Satan also has an avenue to attack Christians from within. That avenue is what the Bible calls **"The Flesh"**. The flesh is our old rebellious sin nature which we are all born with. Its chief goal is always to serve one's self rather than God.

When man fell away from God he immediately developed a sin nature. This nature is a force of rebellion, selfishness and indifference to God. This sin nature, which every person has, attempts to keep us away from depending upon God and instead be completely dependent upon ourselves.

5 | Satan's Attack On Christians

When a person becomes a Christian he does not lose his old sin nature. He does, however, receive a new nature from Christ. This new nature longs to be dependent, unselfish and obedient to God. This new nature from Christ is completely controlled by the Holy Spirit and does what is pleasing to God. The Bible talks about the behavior of these two natures in Romans 8.

ROMANS 8:5-7 (NCV)

5) *Those who live following their sinful selves think only about things that their sinful selves want. But those who live following the Spirit are thinking about the things that the Spirit wants them to do.*

6) *If a person's thinking is controlled by his sinful self, then there is death. But, if his thinking is controlled by the Spirit, then there is life and peace.*

7) *This is true because if a person's thinking is controlled by his sinful self, then he is against God. He refuses to obey God's law. And really he is not able to obey God's law.*

According to verse 5, what does the *"sinful self"* (old nature) do?

_____

_____

_____

Satan's Attack On Christians | 5

According to verse 6 what are the results of following the *"sinful self"*?

_____

_____

_____

According to verse 7 what happens to the person who is controlled by his *"sinful self"*?

_____

_____

_____

According to verse 6 what happens to those who are *"controlled by the Spirit"*?

_____

_____

_____

5 | Satan's Attack On Christians

Satan has an avenue, or a friend, to help him get to us and destroy us. That friend is our sinful nature, or the Flesh. Therefore, the Christian needs to see that he is fighting an inner war over whom he will obey. As the Apostle Paul tells us in Galatians 5, it is a war that can only be won by choosing to obey God's Spirit in the new nature.

GALATIANS 5:17 (NCV)
17) Our sinful selves want what is against the Spirit. The Spirit wants what is against our sinful selves. The two are against each other. So you must not do just what you please.

CONCLUSION

It is very clear that Satan hates Christians because of what God has done for them. He has rescued them from the devil's slavery. He has given them the power to resist his lies. And He has given them the power to save others from his hateful grip. Nevertheless, Satan remains a powerful enemy. Though he no longer owns those who put their faith in Christ, he continues to attack with incredible temptations in hopes that believers will once again turn away from God. However, God, has not left us helpless. In the final two chapters of this manual we will learn about some powerful weapons that God has given us to defend ourselves.

NOTES

6 | The Christian's Armor—Part One

6 The Christian's Armor—Part One

In the last chapter we discussed two ways in which Satan attacks us. He attacks us through the world and he attacks us through the flesh. The question is, what can we do about it? Is it possible for us like Jesus, to withstand the attacks of such a powerful enemy? The answer to that question is a resounding, YES! God has indeed made it possible for us to protect ourselves from the Evil One's attacks. He has given us powerful spiritual armor that, when properly used, will enable us to transform a spiritual attack into a great victory.

> **IN THIS CHAPTER WE WILL LEARN HOW TO PUT ON THE FIRST THREE PIECES OF SPIRITUAL ARMOR WHICH GOD HAS PROVIDED FOR OUR DEFENSE AGAINST SATAN'S ATTACKS.**

EVERY CHRISTIAN NEEDS TO BE PREPARED FOR BATTLE WITH THE RIGHT ARMOR.

A professional soldier would never dream of going to war without the proper equipment. To plunge into a raging battle unprepared would be suicidal. Tragically, many of us as Christians have not yet realized that we too are soldiers in a devastating war. We go out each day to face a brutal enemy. But because we often fail to put on God's protective armor, we struggle home wounded and discouraged. However, the Apostle Paul tells us in Ephesians 6 that God has made it possible for us to protect ourselves from Satan's vicious attacks.

EPHESIANS 6:11-13 (NIV)

11) Put on the full armor of God so that you can take your stand against the devil's schemes.

12) For our struggle is not against flesh and blood, but against the rulers, against the authorities, against the powers of this dark world and against the spiritual forces of evil in the heavenly realms.

13) Therefore put on the full armor of God, so that when the day of evil comes, you may be able to stand your ground, and after you have done everything, to stand.

The Christian's Armor—Part One | 6

According to verse 11 what must we wear to fight off Satan's evil tricks?

_____

_____

_____

According to verse 12 who are we fighting in this spiritual warfare?

_____

_____

_____

According to verse 13 how much of God's armor must we use to stand up to Satan's attacks?

_____

_____

_____

According to verse 13 what is the result when we use God's full armor to defend against Satan's attacks?

_____

_____

_____

From this Scripture it is very clear that Christians have been given all the protection they need to defend themselves from Satan and his evil schemes. We should be very encouraged that God's armor can withstand every spiritual attack. However, just knowing we have the armor is not enough—we must also learn how to use it.

The Apostle Paul lived during the time of the Roman Empire. This great empire had been built by the conquering Roman army. When Paul wrote to the church of Ephesus about the armor of God, he used the image of a Roman soldier as his model. These soldiers were the invincible warriors of their day, but the secret to their success was in their preparation. In much the same way, Ephesians 6:14-15 tells us that we must prepare for our battles by learning to put on our Spiritual Armor.

The Christian's Armor—Part One

6

EPHESIANS 6:14-15 (NIV)
14) Stand firm then, with the belt of truth buckled around your waist, with the breastplate of righteousness in place,
15) and with your feet fitted with the readiness that comes from the gospel of peace.

What three pieces of armor does this passage tell us to put on?

_____

_____

_____

A Roman soldier's belt, breastplate and footwear were far more than just apparel. They were specially-designed to make each warrior more effective on the battlefield. They were also items that would be faithfully put on every day. In fact, when in danger of attack, these well-prepared soldiers would even sleep in this special armor. Let's look more closely at the special protection each item was designed to provide.

The Christian's Armor—Part One

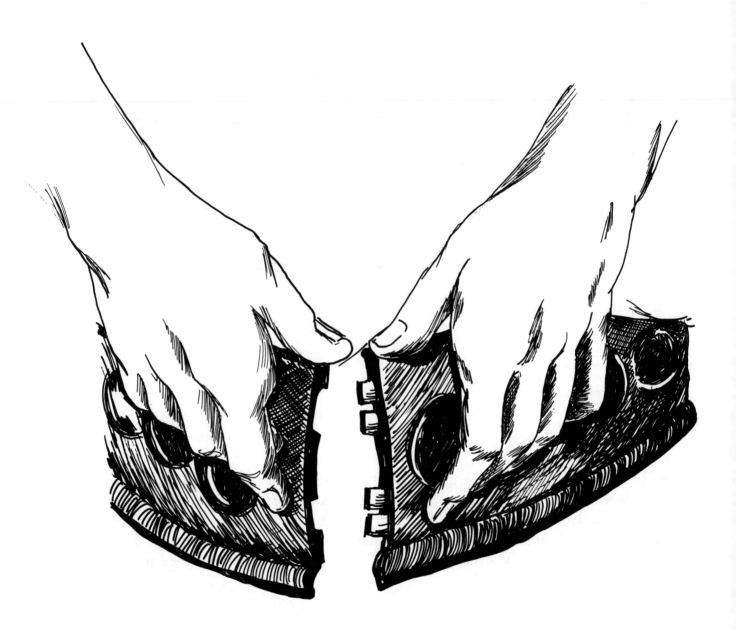

The Christian's Armor—Part One 6

I. THE BELT OF TRUTH

The belt of the Roman soldier was most often a thick leather strap with more than one use. First, it was a utility belt. It could be designed to hold both weapons and tools a warrior would need for combat. Second, it was used to give a soldier complete freedom of movement as he entered a battle. In that day people wore long flowing robes. As you can imagine, trying to run and fight in these robes would be difficult and dangerous. If a warrior were to trip and fall he would become an easy target for his enemy. Therefore, the Roman soldier would pull up the loose ends of his robe and tuck them into his belt. Only when he had done this would he truly be ready to fight. The Bible tells us that we too must buckle on our spiritual belt if we are to be prepared to fight.

EPHESIANS 6:14a (NIV)
14a) Stand firm then, with the belt of truth buckled around your waist...

What do you think *"the belt of truth"* is?

_____

_____

_____

The belt of truth is the knowledge that when we become Christians we operate from a new way of thinking and living that allows us to live a life of dependence on and in obedience to God. This new way of thinking and living is based on the life and teaching of Jesus, who is the Truth. Satan wants us to believe his horrible lie that dependence upon God is death and that we can be happy by being our own god. These and other lies have kept us in bondage, but putting on the belt of truth enable us to reject this self-destructive lie and gain the freedom Jesus offers us in John 8:32.

> JOHN 8:32 (NIV)
> *32) Then you will know the truth, and the truth will set you free.*

What do you think Jesus means when He said *"You will know the truth"*?

_____

_____

_____

Jesus is teaching that we can know reality, that is, we can know the difference between God's Truth and Satan's lies. Since God is the truth, all truth must come from Him.

The Christian's Armor—Part One $\boxed{6}$

What did Jesus mean when He said *"the truth will set you free"*?

_____

_____

_____

It means our lives can become complete and will be complete for all eternity if we will follow God's truth.

EXAMPLES OF TRUTHS THAT MAKE UP THE BELT OF TRUTH

-Man is not made for himself, but for God.
-True life comes from worshipping and serving God.
-Pride and independence from God is the great destroyer of mankind.
-God is holy and just and must punish mankind's sin.
-Only through faith in Christ can mankind be forgiven and have peace with God.
-God calls us to be obedient to Him in the same way Jesus was obedient.

Satan and his demonic forces want to keep Christians from putting on the Belt of Truth. If we don't believe and live the foundational truths of who we are in Christ, we, like the Roman soldier, will trip and fall over Satan's lies and deceptions. Therefore, a Christian who wants to win the battle against Satan must put on the belt of truth.

The Christian's Armor—Part One | 6

II. THE BREASTPLATE OF RIGHTEOUSNESS

The second piece of armor that was absolutely essential for the soldier to wear was his breastplate. The breastplate was often made of strong metal shaped to fit a soldier's upper body. Its purpose was to protect the vital organs of the warrior's chest and stomach from his opponent's weapons. If a soldier could successfully land a blow upon an enemy who was not wearing a breastplate, he could seriously wound or even kill him. In Ephesians 6:14 the Bible tells us that Christians must also put on a breastplate if they are to protect themselves from Satan's deadly attacks.

> EPHESIANS 6:14 (NIV)
> *14) Stand firm then, with the belt of truth buckled around your waist, with the breastplate of righteousness in place,*

What do you think the *"breastplate of righteousness"* is?

_____

_____

_____

The breastplate of righteousness is the very righteousness of Christ which is given to us when we accept Him as our Savior. Christ's righteousness is His complete purity and perfection before God.

How do you think the *"breastplate of righteousness"* protects us?

_____

_____

_____

Guilt is a terrible weapon which Satan uses to strike at a Christian's spiritual heart. He knows that if we feel guilty and unforgiven before God, we will tend to withdraw from Him in shame. Since Satan understands that he cannot really turn God away from us, he does the next best thing—he tries to turn us away from God. By accusing us of sin he makes us feel unworthy of God's love and acceptance.

The Bible tells us that when we put our faith in Christ, God justifies us. That is, He declares us as righteous as Christ. Because we are declared as righteous as Christ, we are always totally accepted by and completely pleasing to God. No matter how much guilt and shame Satan attempts to create with his vicious accusations, we can have full confidence that we are as holy, accepted and pleasing to God as Jesus Himself.

Lawyer

The Christian's Armor—Part One

III. THE SHOES OF THE GOSPEL OF PEACE

The special footwear of the Roman soldier was absolutely essential for battle. It was a sandal strapped tightly around the foot and ankle with numerous leather bands. It provided excellent support for running and fighting. In addition, there were metal cleats or spikes on the sole of the shoe designed to give maximum traction. This piece of armor gave the soldier a solid, firm footing in the midst of battle. The Bible tells us in Ephesians 6:15 that Christians also need the right footwear to help defend against Satan's attacks.

EPHESIANS 6:14-15 (NIV)
14) Stand firm then, with the belt of truth buckled around your waist, with the breastplate of righteousness in place,
15) AND WITH YOUR FEET FITTED WITH THE READINESS THAT COMES FROM THE GOSPEL OF PEACE.

What do you think *"the Gospel of peace"* is?

_____

_____

_____

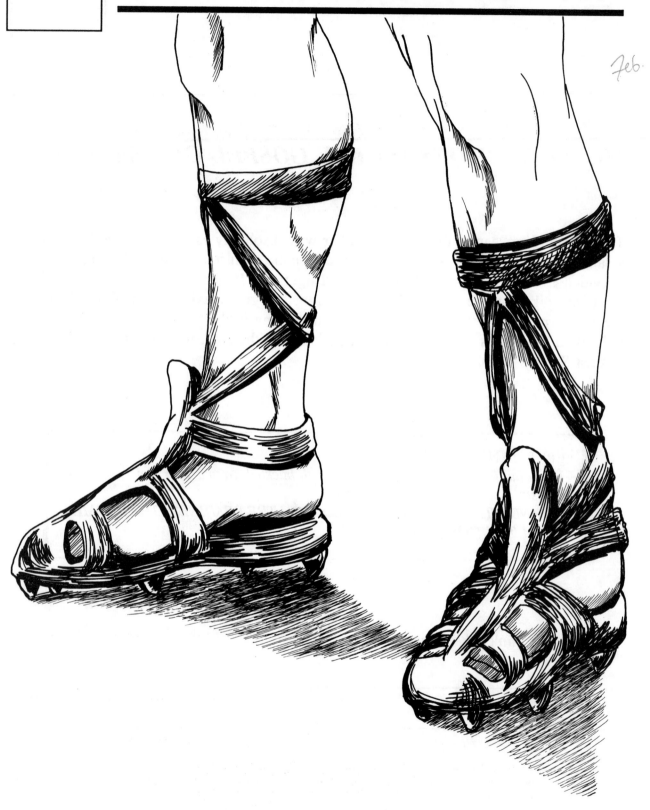

The Christian's Armor—Part One

The gospel of peace is actually two very powerful gifts that God has given to all Christians. The first gift is that God made complete and total peace with us through Christ's death on the cross. In other words, God has forgiven our sins, holds no grudge against us, is our best friend and is always on our side. These things are true because Christ, through His death, paid for every sin—past, present, or future—that could ever separate us from God.

The second gift of the gospel of peace comes when we realize that we are accepted by God. This realization gives us a deep sense of well-being or peace that will never leave us. The Bible reassures us that we can experience this peace even during Satan's most deadly attacks.

PHILIPPIANS 4:6-7 (NCV)
6) Do not worry about anything. But pray and ask God for everything you need. And when you pray, always give thanks.
7) And God's peace will keep your hearts and minds in Christ Jesus. The peace that God gives is so great that we cannot understand it.

According to Philippians 4:6-7, what must we do to experience peace even in the midst of Satan's attacks?

_____

_____

_____

The Roman soldier had to strap on his fighting sandals each day to give himself good footing in battle. In a similar way, we must strap on the truth about the gift of God's peace. We do this by reminding ourselves that God has made peace with us, that He is in control and that He is on our side. What a comfort to know that no matter how rough things get we can have the peace of Christ in our hearts and minds.

SUMMARY

God wants us to realize that we are indeed His soldiers in the Great War. But He also wants us to know that He has given us the protection we need to withstand even Satan's most blistering attacks. In this chapter we learned how to put on and use God's first three pieces of armor—**the belt of truth, the breastplate of righteousness, and the shoes of peace.** In the next chapter we will learn about three more pieces of God's armor—armor that will give us all the protection and power we need to be victorious soldiers of Christ.

The Christian's Armor—Part Two

7 The Christian's Armor—Part Two

God is a mighty warrior. He's the undisputed Victor in the war against Satan. And God wants us as His soldiers to be victorious too. Therefore, He has given us spiritual armor to wear in our battle against Satan. In the last chapter we learned about the belt of truth, the breastplate of righteousness and the shoes of peace. These pieces of armor are critical in our battle against Satan, but the Bible says there are three more pieces of armor which we must use if we are to stand against Satan and his demonic forces.

> **IN THIS DISCUSSION WE WILL LEARN HOW TO PUT ON THE FINAL THREE PIECES OF SPIRITUAL ARMOR IN ORDER TO STAND FIRM AGAINST SATAN'S ATTACKS.**

The Christian's Armor—Part Two

In Ephesians 6:16-17 the Apostle Paul clearly describes the final three pieces of God's armor.

EPHESIANS 6:16-17 (NIV)
16) In addition to all this, take up the shield of faith, with which you can extinguish all the flaming arrows of the evil one.
17) Take the helmet of salvation and the sword of the Spirit, which is the word of God.

According to Ephesians 6:16-17 what are the three pieces of armor we must *"take up"*?

_____

_____

_____

Why do you think these three pieces of armor would be important in protecting yourself against Satan?

_____

_____

_____

Let's take a closer look at the special protection each of these three pieces of armor are designed to provide.

The Christian's Armor—Part Two | 7

I. THE SHIELD OF FAITH

In the time of the Roman Empire, soldiers at war used many tactics that were violent and brutal. For example, these warriors often shot arrows tipped with flaming pitch. Upon impact, the burning tar would splatter, inflicting painful wounds on their opponents. To guard against these attacks, certain Roman soldiers would carry a shield of tough leather or metal. This shield was about 4½ feet high and 2½ feet wide. While under attack, the soldier would simply crouch behind his shield and the flaming missiles would be deflected or extinguished.

Satan is also a violent and brutal enemy. It is his intent to inflict as much pain and destruction on the lives of Christians as possible. His "flaming missiles" include such things as lies, discouragement, fear, lust, and all that a godless world has to offer. But, the Bible says that we have a powerful shield that will protect us from Satan's cruel and deadly arrows.

EPHESIANS 6:16 (NIV)
16) In addition to all this, take up the shield of faith, with which you can extinguish all the flaming arrows of the evil one.

What do you think the *"shield of faith"* is?

_____

_____

_____

The Christian's Armor—Part Two

The Christian's Armor—Part Two

The shield of faith is the awesome protection that God gives us against Satan's attacks. This shield is made available to us when we choose by faith to accept and believe that God is truly our Protector. As the shield of the Roman soldier was large enough to protect him from head to toe, so God, our Shield of Faith, offers us total protection from Satan's attacks. In fact, the Bible has much to say about God's protection.

PSALM 5:12 (TLB)
12) For you bless the godly man, O Lord; you protect him with your shield of love.

PROVERBS 30:5 (TLB)
5) Every word of God proves true. He defends all who come to him for protection.

Why do you think Psalm 5:12 calls God's shield a *"shield of love"*?

_____

_____

_____

According to Proverbs 30:5 what do you think it means to come to God for protection?

_____

_____

We take up the shield of faith when we choose to believe the promises that God has for us. The following Scriptures contain many promises that are part of our *"shield of faith"* from God. Read these verses and list the promises of protection in each.

ROMANS 8:31 (NIV)
31) What, then, shall we say in response to this? If God is for us, who can be against us?

What is the promise?

_____

_____

ROMANS 8:38-39 (NIV)
38) For I am convinced that neither death nor life, neither angels nor demons, neither the present nor the future, nor any powers,
39) neither height nor depth, nor anything else in all creation, will be able to separate us from the love of God that is in Christ Jesus our Lord.

What is the promise?

_____

_____

The Christian's Armor—Part Two

> ROMANS 8:28 (NIV)
> *28) And we know that in all things Gods works for the good of those who love him, who have been called according to his purpose.*

What is the promise?

_____

_____

> I CORINTHIANS 10:13 (NIV)
> *13) No temptation has seized you except what is common to man. And God is faithful; he will not let you be tempted beyond what you can bear. But when you are tempted, he will also provide a way out so that you can stand up under it.*

What is the promise?

_____

_____

> HEBREWS 10:17 (NIV)
> 17) ... "Their sins and lawless acts I will remember no more."

What is the promise?

_____

_____

> PSALMS 46:1 (NIV)
> 1) God is our refuge and strength, an ever-present help in trouble.

What is the promise?

_____

_____

The Christian's Armor—Part Two

> PHILIPPIANS 1:6 (NCV)
> *6) God began doing a good work in you. And he will continue it until it is finished when Jesus Christ comes again. I am sure of that.*

What is the promise?

_____

_____

When we "take up the shield of faith" we are telling Satan by faith that he cannot separate us from God. As we trust God to see us through our trials and remain dependent upon Him, He becomes our Protective Shield against all of Satan's attacks.

II. *THE HELMET OF SALVATION*

One of the most vulnerable parts of the human body is the head. It is the control center for all of our thoughts and actions. For a soldier a head injury had to be avoided at all costs because even a minor wound could cloud his thinking and make him useless on the battlefield. Therefore, a warrior in the Roman army would never fail to protect his head by putting on a strong helmet. The Bible tells us about the helmet that Christians need to wear in Ephesians 6:17.

EPHESIANS 6:17a (NIV)
17a) Take the helmet of salvation...

What do you think *"the helmet of Salvation"* is?

_____

_____

_____

The Christian's Armor—Part Two

7 | The Christian's Armor—Part Two

The helmet of salvation is our belief that when God saved us, His salvation was strong enough to deliver us from the power of Satan's Kingdom and to force him to flee. While a military helmet is designed to protect a soldier's head, the Helmet of Salvation is designed to protect a Christian's mind. As we saw in Chapter 2, Satan's most devastating attack on Adam and Eve was on their minds. He convinced Eve that God's truth was a lie and his own lies were the truth. He now wants us to believe that our salvation is still not strong enough to save us from his power. However, in Colossians 1:13 the Apostle Paul answers this lie.

COLOSSIANS 1:13 (NCV)
13) God has made us free from the power of darkness, and he brought us into the kingdom of his dear Son.

According to Verse 13, under what power were we before Christ rescued us?

_____

_____

_____

The Christian's Armor—Part Two | 7

Because we have received salvation, where are we now?

_____

_____

_____

The Bible is clear that our salvation is not only strong enough to save us from Satan's power, but as we can see in James 4, is also strong enough to cause Satan to flee.

> JAMES 4: 7 (NCV)
> 7) So give yourselves to God. Stand against the devil, and the devil will run away from you.

What do you think it means to *"give yourselves to God"*?

_____

_____

_____

According to verse 7, if we do stand against Satan what will he do?

_____

_____

_____

Satan would like to confuse every Christian about his salvation. He wants us to feel unloved by God and unworthy to be in His Kingdom. If Satan is successful at getting us to believe these lies then we will become discouraged and depressed and our service for Christ will become ineffective. But, when we reject these doubts by firmly believing that Christ has saved us, that He loves us and that He will never leave us, then we have defeated these lies by putting on the Helmet of Salvation. When the helmet of salvation is firmly in place, our mind is well protected so that we can stand against Satan.

The Christian's Armor—Part Two

III. THE SWORD OF THE SPIRIT

As we have seen, a battle-ready Roman soldier had many pieces of armor. When these were used together he was highly protected from enemy attacks. However, the goal of a Roman army was not merely protection, but Victory! To gain this victory a soldier must also be prepared to attack his enemy.

The Roman army used many different kinds of weapons. Spears and bows were very common. But, perhaps the most powerful weapon of a fully-armed Roman warrior was his sword. Usually, this was a short two-edged sword allowing the soldier to respond quickly to an attacker. In the Roman world the sword was a symbol of power and fear to all of the empires enemies. Ephesians 6 tells us that God has also armed Christians with a powerful sword.

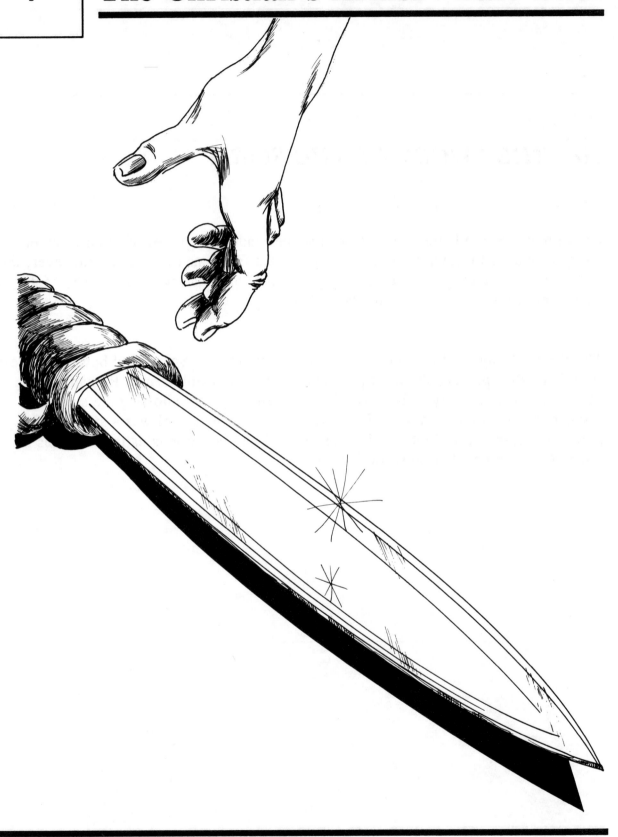

The Christian's Armor—Part Two $\boxed{7}$

EPHESIANS 6:17 (NIV)
17) *Take the helmet of salvation AND THE SWORD OF THE SPIRIT, WHICH IS THE WORD OF GOD.*

According to Ephesians 6:17 what is *"the sword of the Spirit"*?

_____

_____

_____

Why do you think Ephesians 6:17 calls the Word of God a *"sword"*?

_____

_____

_____

7 | The Christian's Armor—Part Two

Nothing cuts through Satan's lies like God's Word. Since Satan is the father of lies, his ability to subtly deceive Christians is nothing short of phenomenal. No Christian alone could stand up to these lies. But, God's Word, with its direct truthfulness slashes like a sword through every lie Satan attempts to push upon us. As we saw in Chapter 3, no one could stand up to Satan like Jesus Christ. When Satan attacked with his lies, Christ always answered with the powerful truth of Scripture. We must also be equipped with the knowledge and truth of Scripture if we are to cut through Satan's lies.

Satan is constantly lying to us as Christians about what will make us happy. The sword, the Word of God, attacks these lies and shows us where real happiness is found. For example:

-Satan wants me to believe that spending my time dwelling on lust will make me happier; **but the Word of God says...**

PHILIPPIANS 4:8 (NCV)
8) Brothers, continue to think about the things that are good and worthy of praise. Think about the things that are true and honorable and right and pure and beautiful and respected.

The Christian's Armor—Part Two

-Satan wants me to believe that if I am my own God and depend on my own reasoning I will be happier; **but the Word of God says...**

> PROVERBS 3:5-6 (NCV)
> *5) Trust the Lord with all your heart. Don't depend on your own understanding.*
> *6) Remember the Lord in everything you do. And he will give you success.*

-Satan tells me not to worry about discipline and hard work, but just relax, be lazy and I'll be happy; **but the Word of God says...**

> MATTHEW 16:24-26 (NCV)
> *24) Then Jesus said to his followers, "If anyone wants to follow me, he must say 'no' to the things he wants. He must be willing even to die on a cross, and he must follow me.*
> *25) Whoever wants to save his life will give up true life. And whoever gives up his life for me will have true life.*
> *26) It is worth nothing for a man to have the whole world if he loses his soul. He could never pay enough to buy back his soul.*

The Christian's Armor—Part Two

-Satan tells me that because I am young, I should not
be concerned with God, but only with the
pleasures of youth; **but the Word of God says...**

ECCLESIASTES 12:1 (NCV)
*1) Remember your Creator while you are young. Your old age is coming when
you will have many troubles. When that time comes, you won't have much to
enjoy.*

-Satan wants me to believe that no one will care about
the gospel so why should I share my faith; **but
the Word of God says...**

MARK 16:15 (NCV)
*15) Jesus said to the followers, "Go everywhere in the world. Tell the Good
News to everyone."*

-Satan wants me to believe that I will be happier if my closest friends are non-Christians; **but the Word of God says...**

II TIMOTHY 2:22 (NCV)
22) Stay away from the evil things young people love to do. Try hard to live right and to have faith, love, and peace. Work for these things together with those who have pure hearts and who trust in the Lord.

The Christian who is serious about winning spiritual warfare must learn how to use the Sword of the Spirit. It is the only weapon God has provided to cut down all of Satan's lies. Only by making God's Word a regular part of our lives will we become the warriors we need to be.

SUMMARY

In this manual we have learned that God created Satan as His most beautiful and most powerful angel. But, because of Satan's pride, he rebelled and tried to become his own god. That was the beginning of a great war between God and Satan. We have also learned that we are caught in the middle of this war. Mankind became Satan's slaves when Adam and Eve accepted his lie that independence from God is life and dependence upon God is death.

However, God in His great love rescued us from our slavery to Satan through Jesus Christ. Jesus exposed Satan's lies by living a life of total dependence upon the Father. Then Jesus totally defeated Satan when He chose to pay the penalty for all of mankind's sin and rebellion by dying on the cross.

Though Satan is totally defeated he still hates Christians and is trying desperately to deceive us. He is constantly tempting us to rebel against God through our own sin nature called the Flesh and through his evil system of values called the World. But God, in His great love for us, has given us special spiritual armor. When we use this armor properly, all of Satan's schemes to defeat us are useless. Best of all, God's full armor will enable us to be warriors who can rescue others from the great war as we share our faith in Christ, and live a life of dependence on and obedience to God.

The Christian's Armor—Part Two

NOTES

_____

_____

_____

_____

_____

_____

_____

_____

_____

_____

_____

_____

_____

A Final Word—
How To Be A Warrior In Prayer

We have learned much in this book about how to be a warrior in the great spiritual war. Ephesians 6:10-17 taught us a great deal about who the real enemy is (Satan) and how to be victorious against him (putting on the spiritual armor).

However, in Ephesians 6:18 God tells us about another powerful and important weapon to use in our warfare.

Ephesians 6:18 (NIV)
18) And pray in the Spirit on all occasions with all kinds of prayers and requests. With this in mind, be alert and always keep on praying for all the saints.

According to Ephesians 6:18 when should we pray and who should we pray for?

_____

_____

_____

What kinds of prayers does verse 18 tell us to pray?

_____

_____

_____

God has provided us with strong and complete armor, but He wants us to strengthen this armor through prayer. He wants us to understand that when we put on the armor with prayer we are warriors with incredible power. The Apostle Paul tells us about this power in II Corinthians 10:3-4.

II Corinthians 10:3-4 (NCV)
3) We do live in the world. But we do not fight in the same way that the world fights.
4) We fight with weapons that are different from those the world uses. Our weapons have power from God. These weapons can destroy the enemy's strong places....

Satan is constantly trying to build "strong places" in our lives and in the lives of our friends. A repeated struggle with doubts about faith, or with the same sin, or with frequent failure may really be Satan's "strong places" in our lives. II Corinthians 10:4 clearly tells us that God's *"weapons can destroy the enemy's strong places."* The following prayer project can help you discover how powerful God's weapons are.

PUTTING ON YOUR ARMOR WITH PRAYER

Pray this prayer one time each day for a week. After the first couple of days you may want to add in *specific* needs for yourself and others. After the first week change the prayer to fit your own personality. The important thing is to keep praying and keep believing that your prayers really are powerful weapons that God uses against Satan.

Dear Father,

You have told me to put on your full armor so that I can stand against Satan's attacks. Thank you for giving me this special spiritual protection.

I'm sorry for the times I have tried to depend on myself alone. I know this can only lead to failure. Thank you for allowing me to depend on you and your mighty armor. Father, I really do believe in it, and I want to learn more and more about how to use it.

Therefore, by faith, I want to put on your full armor right now:

As I buckle on the *belt of truth* teach me to see myself and my world through your eyes and not be deceived by Satan's lies.

As I put on the *breastplate of righteousness* help me to understand that I am as righteous to you as Jesus Himself.

As I lace up the *shoes of the gospel of peace*, cause me to realize that you have allowed me to make total peace with you and that I can bring your peace to others.

As I pick up the *shield of faith* remind me that your protection completely surrounds me, even during Satan's most vicious attacks.

As I put on the *helmet of salvation* make me clearly see that, through Christ's death, my life has been bought and paid for, that I now belong to you and that Satan can never own me again.

As I take up the *sword of the spirit* which is your Word, cause me to never forget that there is truth in the Bible to defeat every lie Satan may ever try to tell me.

Father, thank you for making me a mighty warrior in your army. And thank you for teaching me how prayer can turn your armor into powerful spiritual weapons. You have promised me that these weapons will destroy Satan's strong places. Help me to remember that by prayer I can use these weapons each day for the needs in my life and for the needs in the lives of my friends.

I know that Jesus has already defeated Satan by being totally dependent on You in both His life and His death. Teach me to do the same. Thank You that I am on the Winning Side. In Jesus Name. Amen.

ABOUT SHEPHERD MINISTRIES

Shepherd Ministries is an organization meeting the needs of youth and serving as a resource to church youth groups through several different areas:

- **Publications** — With the writing skill of Dawson McAllister and others, Shepherd offers youth resource manuals for spiritual growth and maturity. Currently fifteen books are published to assist youth in their relationships with God, parents, and others. Leaders' guides are available for many of these topics. Beyond the written page, Shepherd produces videos which touch the the pulse of the American student. Whether the topic concerns one's self-esteem, how to get along with parents, or any other of the thirteen topics, the videos capture the attention of the student culture. The latest product, "Life 101: Learning To Say 'YES' to Life!" is a two-part video designed for the public school. Part one was purposely made for general assemblies and describes the problem of teenage suicide. Part two, to be shown outside of class time, gives the ultimate answer in Jesus Christ. For a list of publications offered by Shepherd, locate the order form found in the back of this book.

- **Student Conferences** — The backbone of Shepherd is the weekend conferences held in the larger cities of the nation. With the ministry of music and praise from Todd Proctor, Al Holley and others, and the teaching of Dawson McAllister, students eagerly attend these memorable events. This past year over 82,000 students attended these weekend events.

- **Youth Minister Conference** — A weeklong conference presently held during the fall in Dallas, this event is designed to minister to the youth pastor or worker and spouse. "Youth Ministry" is a joint venture of Shepherd Ministries and Rapha, and seeks to encourage, challenge, and assist youth ministers and their spouses.

- **Parent Seminar** — "Preparing Your Teenager for Sexuality" video seminar. Available to churches as a one-day event, Dawson teaches this seminar via giant screen video. Aaron Shook, a Christian singer/songwriter, leads the seminar and provides live music. This seminar equips parents with a step-by-step method for teaching kids God's view of sex. "Preparing Your Teenager for Sexuality" is also available as a stand-alone video series.

- **Television** — Dawson McAllister's mission is to reach the American student. Though many will not darken the door of a church, all of them will turn the dial of a television. A series of three prime-time tv specials were produced and aired in 22 of the largest cities in America to reach those students. In Dallas in 1989 the program, "Too Young To Die" took first place in the Neilsen ratings for that evening hour.

- **Radio** — The newest tool to reach the American teenager is live call-in radio entitled, "Dawson McAllister Live." This one-hour weekly satellite program brings troubled, confused teenagers into contact with straight talk and clear Biblical guidance. Each student who calls and receives Dawson's compassionate counsel on the air represents thousands of others with similar problems. Not only do they hear Dawson's advice, but the students are invited to call for one-on-one counseling on a toll-free line.

More From Dawson McAllister and Shepherd Ministries...

STUDENT MANUALS FROM DAWSON
A Walk With Christ To The Cross
A Walk With Christ Through The Resurrection
Discussion Manual For Student Relationships Vols. I, II, III
Discussion Manual For Student Discipleship Vols. I, II
Student Conference Follow-up Manual
Search For Significance
Student Conference Follow-up Manual
The Great War
Who Are You, God?
Who Are You, Jesus?
You, God, And Your Sexuality

VIDEOS FROM DAWSON
A Walk With Christ To The Cross
Christianity In Overalls
Dawson Speaks Out On Self-Esteem And Loneliness
How To Know You're In Love
How To Get Along With Your Parents
Life 101- Learning To Say Yes! To Life
Papa, Please Love Me
Preparing Your Teenager For Sexuality
Straight Talk About Friends And Peer Pressure
Tough Questions About Sex
When Tragedy Strikes
Why R.U.? - The Why and Way Out of Substance Abuse

TEACHER MANUALS FROM DAWSON
A Walk With Christ To The Cross
Discussion Manual For Student Relationships Vols. I, II, III
Preparing Your Teenager For Sexuality
The Great War
Who Are You, God?
Who Are You, Jesus?

BOOKS FROM DAWSON
Please Don't Tell My Parents: Answers For Kids In Crises

MUSIC FROM SHEPHERD
Begin With Praise Again - Al Holley
Everything Under The Son - Todd Proctor
Higher And Higher - Al Holley
Love Starts Here - Al Holley
Power Up: Praise For Youth - Todd Proctor
Power Up: Praise And Worship Kit - Todd Proctor
We Stand As One - Todd Proctor
We Stand As One: Praise and Worship Kit - Todd Proctor

OTHER SHEPHERD MINISTRIES PRODUCTS
A Safe Place - Jan Morrison
Brand Name Christians - Mike Worley
Cartoon Clip-Art For Youth Leaders Vols. I, II - Ron Wheeler
Search For Significance - Robert McGee

_____ **YES!** Please Send Me a _FREE_ copy of your latest product catalog.

Name_____

Church_____

Street Address_____

City/State/Zip_____

Phone Number_____

For More Information Or To Order Any Of These Products Contact:
Shepherd Ministries
2845 W. Airport Frwy. / Suite 137
Irving, TX. 75062
(214) 570-7599
FAX (214) 257-0632